Look
Great
Feel
Great

Look Great Feel Great

12 Keys to Enjoying a Healthy Life Now

JOYCE MEYER

Faith Words

NEW YORK BOSTON NASHVILLE

All scripture quotations, unless otherwise indicated, are taken from The Amplified Bible (AMP). The Amplified Bible, Old Testament. Copyright © 1965, 1987 by The Zondervan Corporation. The Amplified New Testament, copyright © 1954, 1958, 1987 by The Lockman Foundation. Used by permission.

Scripture quotations marked "NKJV" are taken from the New King James Version. Copyright © 1982 by Thomas Nelson, Inc. Used by permission. All rights reserved.

Scripture quotations marked "NIV" are taken from The Holy Bible, New International Version®. NIV®. Copyright © 1973, 1978, 1984 by International Bible Society. Used by permission of Zondervan Publishing House. All rights reserved.

Scripture quotations marked "The Message" are taken from The Message. Copyright © 1993, 1994, 1995, 1996, 2000, 2001, 2002. Used by permission of NavPress Publishing Group.

FaithWords
Hachette Book Group USA
237 Park Avenue
New York, NY 10017

Visit our Web site at www.faithwords.com

Printed in the United States of America

Originally published in hardcover by Hachette Book Group USA.

First Trade Edition: November 2008
10 9 8 7 6 5 4 3 2 1

FaithWords is a division of Hachette Book Group USA, Inc. The FaithWords name and logo are trademarks of Hachette Book Group USA, Inc.

The Library of Congress has cataloged the hardcover edition as follows:
Meyer, Joyce.
Look great, feel great : 12 keys to enjoying a healthy life now / Joyce Meyer.—1st ed.
p. cm.
ISBN-13: 978-0-446-57946-9 (regular ed.)
ISBN-10: 0-446-57946-7 (regular ed.)
ISBN-13: 978-0-446-57983-4 (lg. print ed.)
ISBN-10: 0-446-57983-1 (lg. print ed.)
1. Health—Religious aspects—Christianity. I. Title.
BT732.M49 2006
248.4—dc22   2005034324

ISBN 978-0-446-50491-1 (pbk.)

Contents

Contents

Introduction

Do you have any idea how valuable you are? If you suffer from self-doubt or self-hatred, if you abuse your body with bad food or bad habits, even if you simply put yourself at the very bottom of the list of people you do things for, under the kids and spouse and parents and boss and friends, then you do *not* understand your own value. If you did, you wouldn't treat yourself that way. You were put on this earth to spread God's love, and nothing could be more valuable than that.

Maybe you never learned your own importance. That's what happened to me. As a child, I was abused and came to believe that I was the least valuable person on the planet. It took me many years of studying God's word and experiencing fellowship with Him before I got even an inkling of my own worth.

Or maybe you did know your value when you were younger, but somewhere along the way you forgot it, buried it under a to-do list that clamored louder for your attention than your own soul did. If so, then join the club. The degraded value systems in the modern world bombard us with the message that our spirit, soul, and body come last, after money and food and status and stuff. No matter how hard we resist, we all succumb now and then.

I can't tell you how important it is to reform your value system and go back to a much older value system. *God's* value system. It applies to all people, and it puts your entire being (body, mind, will, emotions, and spirit) right at the top of God's list of important and valuable things. Your entire being plays an important role in God's plan; He's entrusted you to take care of it, and that's a lot of responsibility indeed. Only by keeping your spirit, soul, and body in tip-top condition can you truly do God's work.

Let me give you an example. One day I was experiencing a lot of guilt over something I did wrong. Although I asked God to forgive me and believed that He did, I still felt guilty. My mind was on my past when it should have been on my future. I felt depressed and discouraged. I had a headache, and in general did not feel like doing much of anything. The Holy Spirit began to deal with my attitude. He asked me if I thought my attitude was helping me do His work. He then said, "I want you to get over this because you are no good to Me in this condition." The Holy Spirit's straightforward way of dealing with me helped me see that I was wasting my day on negative emotions. I was actually allowing my soul (mind, will, and emotions) to adversely affect my spirit and my body. My spirit felt oppressed and my body ached. We must realize that we are complex creatures and every part of us affects the other parts.

If we don't take good care of our bodies, our spirit and soul will be less effective. If we worry excessively, it can adversely affect our health. If we have no relationship with God and are spiritually weak, nothing seems to work right in our lives. We are definitely tri-part beings and have many facets to our nature, and each needs proper care.

But how do you do spirit maintenance, soul maintenance, and body maintenance? You can't drop them off at the local mechanic for a tune-up. No, but one of the best ways to care for your spirit and soul while on this planet is to care for your body. Your body is the temple of your spirit and soul; it is the house they dwell in while on this earth. God's word says that your body is the temple of God! He dwells in those who believe in Him.

> Do you not know that your body is the temple (the very sanctuary) of the Holy Spirit Who lives within you, Whom you have received [as a Gift] from God? You are not your own.
>
> I Corinthians 6:19

What if you went to a church and it was run-down? Peeling paint, broken doors, smudged windows that didn't let the light in. You'd wonder about the pastor, wouldn't you? The church is his instrument for celebrating the glory of God, yet if he doesn't respect the church enough to take the time to keep it in good condition, what does this say about his relationship with God?

The same question applies to your own body. It's your God-given instrument for experiencing life on Earth and for doing good works. It is the home of your spirit where God dwells. To do the work you were meant to do, you need to keep it in shape. If you let your body get too shabby or sick, it will be a constant distraction. You will not be able to experience the Presence of God and His joy and peace any more than you could in a church building that was uncomfortable, falling apart, or aesthetically demoralizing. Each time we break down emotionally, mentally, or physically, it has a wearing effect on us. If we do it too often, we may eventually come to a place where we can no longer be restored.

I still have to remind myself of this. Once I hurt my voice by speaking in a seminar with an extremely sore throat. That morning when I woke up, I could barely make a sound. I knew I shouldn't speak, but I thought about the disappointment of the audience if I didn't. So I forced myself to speak, thinking I could just get through the day and rest my voice the next day. I was not showing respect for my body and pushed my own needs to the bottom of the pile. I did not use wisdom or common sense.

It seems we often plan to take care of ourselves some other day! I managed to speak that day, but the next day I could not make a sound. I couldn't the next day either, or the day after that. I had to adjust my schedule. The condition continued, and I began to worry. I could tell that something was wrong with my throat. I finally went to the doctor, who told me that I had damaged my vocal cords and that I should never again do public speaking with an extremely sore throat. He gave me medicine to reduce the swelling and inflammation. He said each time we push ourselves beyond reasonable limits, we do some damage, and if we do it too often we get to a point where we can't recover. He said it might reach a point where I could not teach at all if I did not respect my voice and take care of it.

Think about that. By ignoring my body's wisdom and trying to please others at that moment, I nearly jeopardized my entire public ministry! If I had permanently damaged my voice, I would have wound up helping far fewer people and derailing my life's calling. Now I'm more careful about protecting the tools I need to do God's work—my voice, my mind, my heart, emotions and my body. In fact, when you think about it, all your ability to be active and do good in the world requires a healthy mind, body, and soul, and those things rely on a healthy lifestyle and environment. Keeping this big picture in mind can help you stay on your life's path and not make shortsighted decisions.

That's what this book is about. I wrote it because I am dismayed at the number of people I see—at my book signings, in my ministry, and in the general public—who are not taking care of themselves. Many of them clearly feel terrible. Anyone can see this in the way they look and the way they carry themselves. You simply cannot look really great if you don't feel great. How you feel will show up somewhere; in your body language, the dull look in your eyes, or even the tone of your skin. It is in our nature to take care of ourselves, so *why don't we?* I thought about the ways that this can go wrong, and I came up with these reasons:

1. *We don't know how to take care of our physical bodies.* Decades of bad diets, misinformation, and easy access to fast-food and prepackaged food have left people amazingly confused about what a wholesome diet is and how they should eat. You may be surprised at how easy and sensible it is to eat right! I'll give you the information you need to understand how different foods affect you, along with some extremely simple guidelines to follow.

2. *We have a skewed body image planted in our minds by media and advertising.* On one side we are inundated with unattainable

ideals of beauty, while on the other, obesity is so prevalent that it's almost considered the norm. We need to reset our internal picture of what a healthy person should look like.

3. *We have lost touch with exercise.* For virtually all of human existence, exercise was an integral part of our daily existence. Now we've invented enough conveniences that we often live completely divorced from exercise. However, it turns out a good deal of our well-being is dependent on exercise. Once I explain everything that exercise does for you, you may be inspired to make it a daily part of your own life. I'll show you some simple ways to keep in shape that won't turn your schedule topsy-turvy.

4. *We have let ourselves slip into unworkable lives.* With the incredible pressures of juggling career and parenthood, paying steep mortgages and increased fuel prices and burning the proverbial candle at both ends and everywhere in between, it is oh-so-easy to put the workout off. Instead, we'll grab a cheeseburger on the run, cheat our sleep time in order to catch up on paperwork and let the tail wag the dog until we've cut everything out of our lives that once gave us pleasure or kept us sane. This is bad enough, because life is a gift and is meant to be joyful. It should be pleasurable *and* sane. But once you learn the impact of all this stress on your physical health, you will understand what a crime against yourself this is—and, I hope, take action to reclaim a workable life.

5. *Some have become pathologically selfless.* Selflessness can be addictive. It feels so good to do for others and it makes us feel

important. Yes, it is a good thing to help others and should be a major part of our life, but in my line of work, I often see people who routinely ignore their basic needs. The only thing that gives them meaning is doing things for others. This is admirable, but it can easily cross the line into mistaking suffering for virtue. Martyrs usually end up bitter. And once the body breaks down and life is no longer joyful, it becomes increasingly hard to serve anyone. Volunteers in a soup kitchen don't let their pots fall apart while they ladle out one more bowl of soup. They take the time to care for the equipment they need to do their calling. And you should do the same with your most important piece of equipment—your body.

I am not suggesting that we be selfish because that renders us very unhappy and is not how God teaches us to live. We are to live sacrificially and be involved in doing good works, but we must not ignore our own basic needs in the process. Everything in life must be balanced or something breaks down and quite often it is us.

6. We have lost our support. When we don't have a good social network or a godly foundation to keep our spirits high, it becomes easy to slip into boredom, loneliness, and depression. If we aren't able to somehow fill that void, the devil will. You may have heard the saying "Nature abhors a vacuum." Well, let me tell you, the devil loves one! He'll put lots of bad food within easy reach and let you mistake spiritual or emotional hunger for physical hunger. Maintaining a good support network is a terrific way to prevent the formation of bad habits. We need to have the right people around us who will speak up if they see us getting out of balance. We need to spend regular time in fellowship with God and learning His principles. His Holy Spirit who works through His Word convicts us of wrong-doing and gives us the chance to make positive changes before we break down or become ill.

7. *We have forgotten our own value.* This is where I started, and it's the point I come back to. If you don't understand your own importance in the Big Plan, taking care of yourself seems pointless. Reminding you of your place in God's plan is my first and most important task. God has a great future planned for you and you need to be ready for it! You need to look great and feel great, ready to do whatever God asks of you.

My Story

I Corinthians 6:19–20 explains that your body is the temple of the Holy Spirit, Who is in you since you received Him from God. You are not your own property; you have been bought and paid for. That is why you should use your body for the glory of God. God's plan for you involves maintaining a sound mind, body, and soul, as well as a healthy spirit. Yet as I've said, in the modern world it is all too easy to let one, two, or all of these slip. A number of factors work against us. Before you know it, the temple is in shambles and you don't even know how to start the restoration. You may be more tempted to call the whole thing a tear-down.

But that restoration process is a lot simpler than you think. It just involves taking things one step at a time and learning a few secrets along the way. I know, because there was a time in my own life when I would have loved to take the wrecking ball to my own temple. I learned some bad lessons early in life and came to dislike my body, so of course I had little motivation to take care of it, which just made my problems worse. Sad to say, I learned the hard way of how important it is that we take good care of ourselves. The process of restoring my body to health required a genuine commitment, but now that I've achieved health and fitness, I know what a difference it makes. I pay attention to the upkeep of my mind, emotions, body, and spirit, and I'm eager to be the architect for others and help them design a plan for their own restoration project.

My poor relationship with my body began with sexual, emotional, and mental abuse throughout my childhood. My home life was extraordinarily dysfunctional. I lived under constant stress, although I certainly didn't know that term back then. I began to feel the effects of it in my body by the time I was a teenager. The first trouble I remember was constipation and stomach pains. I went to the doctor, who told me that I had a spastic colon. Only years later did I learn that disorder is usually caused by excessive tension, nervousness, and stress. Remember, any time the body cannot relax, that state of "dis-ease" promotes disease.

During those years of abuse and fear, I developed a shame-based nature. I felt bad about myself all the time. Feelings like that can develop into a very dangerous feedback loop, which is exactly what happened to me. Since I didn't like myself, and didn't feel attractive, I had no confidence, and I acted like it. I was twenty pounds overweight because I was eating bad food and not exercising, and I didn't feel that I was special enough to make any kind of effort on my own behalf. I looked bad and felt bad. I was the last girl to get asked out on a date because I didn't feel pretty and wasn't doing anything to help myself. This, of course, just made the feedback loop worse.

Guilt was my constant companion through my teen years. I thought there must be something wrong with me—what else would cause my father to abuse me and treat me like dirt? I grew up as a very insecure adult with low self-esteem. I felt worthless.

Abused children often develop these feelings, but can react to them in different ways. I added more stress to my life by trying to prove I had value through accomplishments. I worked very hard, desperate for approval and fearful that if I did not provide for myself no one else ever would. I also became a rescuer of those in trouble. I had an overdeveloped sense of responsibility and made myself accountable for things I should have let other people handle.

My emotional life was a mess due to the years of mistreatment. I was easily angered, frustrated most of the time, and my mood could swing erratically. Deep down, I felt God was mad at me. Even though I attempted to have a relationship with Him, it was dysfunctional. I did not know how to receive love—His or anyone else's.

Receiving God's unconditional love is the beginning of all emotional healing. Until we can receive that, we cannot love ourselves properly, nor can we love others. I believe the world is love-starved and busy trying to get it through sources that will never satisfy, while God wants to give it freely. Money cannot satisfy. Neither can position, power or fame. All are poor substitutes for love. All leave an inner discontent that causes all kinds of problems, including obesity. People are trying to satisfy a hunger that food cannot relieve.

At the age of eighteen, I married, left home, and moved more than fifteen times during a five-year period. I had no real friends because I never developed any relationships as a child. I didn't know how to make friends and maintain a healthy relationship. I was lonely and sad, which is another kind of love-starved emptiness.

My first marriage was extremely stressful. We separated numerous times. He was a heavy drinker, had trouble keeping a job, had affairs with other women, and was a petty thief. I can't begin to describe just how unstable my life was back then.

I had a miscarriage and later gave birth to a son. When I left the hospital with my baby I had nowhere to go, so I lived with a relative for a few months. After filing for divorce, I moved back to my parents' house in desperation. I'm sure you can see that stress was my normal state. I did not realize that all of this was taking its toll on my body.

I met Dave Meyer when my son was nine months old and we got married after a whirlwind courtship of five dates. Obviously, because of all the internal problems I had, the first several years of our marriage were not peaceful. Had Dave not been a committed Christian, I doubt he would have stayed with me.

Though my relationship with God then was not what I now call healthy, I worked hard at it—as I did at everything. I wanted to help people and God called me into the ministry in 1976 when I was thirty-three years old. As a woman trying to start a new ministry, I experienced opposition from family, friends, and my church. More stress! I threw myself into my ministry full-tilt. It was my way of feeling valuable. My identity was still wrapped up in my accomplishments.

Always dogged by the fear of failure and the sense of worthlessness that accompanied it, I concentrated hard on success. I scheduled as much as I possibly could into every day. Sleep? Relaxation? Fun? Laughter? These were tantamount to wasted time. Besides, I did so much every day and worked so late every night that I could never get my system to slow down enough for much sleep. I fueled myself with coffee every morning to overcome the sleeplessness and keep myself going.

By the time I was thirty-six I started showing more serious symptoms in my body. I got sick for four months straight. I felt so bad most of the time I could hardly get off the couch. I realize now it was because my body was already breaking down due to the years of stress. Later I started having hormone imbalances. My menstrual cycles were too frequent and excessive. I took shots of estrogen every ten days just to function. Eventually I had a hysterectomy, which immediately plunged me into the change of life.

In 1989 I was diagnosed with breast cancer. The tumor was fast-growing and estrogen-dependent, which not only meant I needed immediate surgery but also that I could no longer take hormone-replacement therapy while going through early menopause. I had surgery and endured several more years of sheer misery because my hormonal system was such a mess. As you might imagine, I was a wreck.

During this time my migraine headaches started. They were regular and excruciating. I often felt like a knife was sticking in my right eye.

Despite all of this I continued my work in the ministry. I traveled, taught God's word, stood in faith for my own healing, and often wondered how I could go on much longer. Had you seen me, you might not have known anything was wrong at all. You would have considered me a successful and important woman, like most people did. I looked tired but not sick. Sometimes that was frustrating, because I would tell someone how bad I felt and they would say, "Well, you sure don't look sick." They probably just thought I was "looking my age." They couldn't see that I was so tired inside and out that when I woke up in the morning I wished it was time to go to bed. I did my duty, I worked hard, but I did not enjoy *anything*.

Undoubtedly, part of my problem came from years of dieting. I was always about twenty pounds overweight and always on a fad diet. Like most people who diet all their lives, I probably lost and gained back a thousand pounds. My body didn't know what to expect. And I didn't know what to give it. I grew up on fried foods and starch. No one ever taught me what a body needs to stay healthy. I wanted to lose weight, eat right, look good, and feel good; I just didn't know how.

Eventually I started reading books on nutrition. I firmly believe God led me to them. I learned basic facts that helped me immensely. I learned how important food choices are and how dangerous vitamin deficiencies can be; about protein, fat, and carbohydrates. I finally understood the simple truth of the old saying "you are what you eat." Different foods impact your performance, your health, your feelings, your looks, and the very makeup of your body. I realized that eating right had to be a way of life, not just a diet I used to lose some weight, only to return to bad habits and gain it back. I was tired of that cycle. Many of you are tired as well.

The books I read at that time did not include information on stress. Back then, few scientists understood the strength of the mind-body connection like they do today. They knew stress could make you frazzled, they knew it had a negative effect on your health, but they didn't realize just how sick it could make you. They didn't know it could make you age faster than normal. Plenty of the doctors I saw (and I was always seeing doctors) told me that I was under extreme stress and desperately needed to make some lifestyle changes. They told me I was too emotional, too intense, but what was the solution? I felt like I was trapped. Taking a year off to recover was out of the question. We had a large staff at our ministry and I felt they all depended on me. If I didn't do my part, then nobody got a paycheck. My work was all-consuming; nothing could be dropped or delegated. This is a classic illusion we all fall for from time to time. Sometimes we prefer to stay confused rather than face the truth and deal with the issues in our lives. When people who loved me tried to tell me that I needed to stop working so hard, I just told them they didn't understand my calling.

During this time, I didn't understand why God was not protecting my health. Here I was, doing His work, and He wasn't helping me be well so I could do it better. I blamed a lot of my ill health on the devil. I believed he was throwing obstacles in my path because I tried to help people. I was right—he was derailing me—but I finally realized that the only reason he could was because I threw a door wide open for him to come into my life. I was breaking God's laws of health and rest and He wasn't giving me a special pass that excused me from reaping what I was sowing.

No matter what our reason for abusing ourselves, when we

do this, we sow seeds of disobedience and they will always bring a harvest of physical, mental, and emotional breakdown. The Apostle Paul worked with a man who got sick from working too hard in ministry. The man almost died, but the Lord spared him and Paul sent him home. I think it is interesting that he did not go straight back to work. He went home to rest!

For years, while my ministry grew and flourished, I was constantly sick. It was rarely completely debilitating, but it was one small thing after another. I never, ever felt truly well. My body tried to tell me something, but I didn't listen.

I took nutritional supplements, and I believe they helped me survive—more than any medicines I was given! I thanked God more than once for vitamins, minerals, herbs, protein shakes, and energy drinks. But my body was so depleted of health that all the supplements did was shore me up and get me out there for another day. I never built any nutritional reserves, and the stress just kept sucking out everything I put in. Stressed bodies use tremendous amounts of nutrients. People who have barely enough energy to get through each day have no reserves.

I finally came to a point where I was so depleted that if anything stressful happened I would experience shortness of breath and break into a sweat, even something as mundane as suddenly stepping on my brakes in traffic. I cried easily. My body and emotions felt completely alien to me. When my blood pressure hit a dangerous peak, I knew it was time to make some changes and the only one who could do it was me.

I eliminated a lot of stress from my life by cutting things from my schedule that weren't bearing any fruit. This sounds easy, but it was very hard. After all, I was in charge of an international ministry and felt I needed to be involved in everything that happened. Have you ever felt that if you don't stay in-volved, nothing will be done right? Is it hard for you to delegate tasks to others? If so, I know how you feel, but I can also tell you that as long as you keep that attitude, your work will never get done and you will probably feel stressed out and joyless.

I decided that even if a job wasn't accomplished the exact way I preferred, it was better for me to delegate to others. You'll be amazed at how others will grow into a role when given the space to do so! Trust is an empowering emotion. Besides, what's the point in doing everything yourself if the stress makes you feel so lousy that you can't enjoy the fruits of your labor?

But my body was way beyond the place where simply dele-gating responsibility was going to get me back to health. I liter-ally could not relax my muscles. I had no idea that unbelievably tight neck muscles were behind my migraine headaches. I spoke at a church in Florida and once again had a terrible headache. The pastor suggested I let a physical therapist in the church massage my neck. I thought to myself, "What good can that do? I'm sick—rubbing my neck won't fix it." But I reluc-tantly agreed. When the woman touched my neck, I practically jumped out of my skin. My neck was so tight and sore that I could barely stand for her to touch it. She encouraged me to bear with it and let her work the tightness out of my muscles.

To my astonishment, my headache stopped. That was my introduction to massage, and believe me, I got as many as I could after that. Massage helps relax the body, circulates blood to the skin surface, pushes toxins out of the muscles, helps skin tone, and brings a sense of well-being to the whole body. I'll explain more about the therapeutic benefits of massage later in this book.

Although massage helped me immensely, I found that because I still had not eliminated the stress from my life, I made no permanent progress. The massages relaxed me, but by the end of the next day all my muscles were tight again.

When I finally combined nutritional help with positive lifestyle changes like massage and a more relaxed schedule, I started seeing good results. I achieved some muscle relaxation, which helped eliminate headaches and neck and back pain. I also experienced an increase in my energy level. But this didn't happen overnight! I abused my body for a long time—my entire life, really—and it took almost three years before I felt really good.

Don't be scared by that three-year time frame! My health improved gradually, all along the way, and just receiving a taste of being better is a powerful motivator. What's it like when you have been sick and then you start to get better? There is something joyful in that, even if you aren't completely well. My process of recovery was rewarding, but it took time. Don't think that you can take two things off your schedule, swallow some vitamins every day, and instantly be well.

Your recovery may not take as long as mine, or it could take longer. It all depends on how bad your condition is. But, no matter how long it takes, now is the time to begin. Don't settle for feeling bad one more day while you do nothing about it but complain. There is help! Your body has the ability to restore itself. God will work in you to bring you back to wholeness if you follow His guidelines for good health. In the Bible, Proverbs 18:14 states that the strong spirit of a man will sustain him in bodily pain or trouble. If you are ready to follow God's plan for wholeness and be spirit-led, the rest will follow.

I wrote *Look Great, Feel Great* because I can truthfully say that I feel better physically, mentally, emotionally, and spiritually right now than I ever have in my life. That's a big claim! I live every day passionately, and what a breathtaking change that is. Too many of us get trapped in a rut of negative thinking, believing our healthiest days are behind us and that we will simply get more out of shape, sicker, and less energetic as we age. I'm living proof that's not so! These are my best days. I have an energy and contentment I've never known, a fierce faith, and I fully expect to live out my life in health and grace. No matter what age or condition you are, you can do the same. We have a promise from God that we can still be very productive in old age, and I want to help you get there.

> [Growing in grace] they shall still bring forth fruit in old age; they shall be full of sap [of spiritual vitality] and [rich in the] verdure [of trust, love, and contentment].
>
> Psalm 92:14

Over the years I have learned how to take care of myself and most of all I have learned that I can have a lifetime of health for my body and soul. I want to share with you my thoughts, knowledge, experience, and encouragement. I want to share my faith with you also, because I believe good health for the whole person requires a solid faith in God through Jesus Christ. He helped me through all the rough years and He restored me. God showed me what to do and led me to make positive changes. Sometimes it took me a long time to fully obey, but I can say from experience that God's ways work. His word is filled with guidelines for good health; any person who follows them will experience good results. I want to save you the time it took me to comprehend them. It took me many, many years to get it straight!

What that means is that I have been in some deep, dark places where I could see no light at all. I started my life in such a place. I know how hopeless it can seem, and I wouldn't be telling you that taking care of the little things can make the big things come true if I hadn't been there and done it myself. I was the lonely, depressed, and overweight girl; I was the workaholic; I was ill with stress; I was addicted to caffeine and cigarettes; I felt lost and like I was wandering in a spiritual desert; I was the chronic dieter.

I was all those things, each and every one, and it felt overwhelming and insurmountable, but I have seen God deliver me from all those troubles once I achieved clarity and made the decision to concentrate on the basics. I do the little things each day to care for my body and soul, and let God be my constant companion on this journey. Now I feel great, I accomplish more than ever before, reach more people, and do it all with the joy, passion, and freedom that God intended us to live with every day. It's your birthright to have this, and I hope you'll join with me as we take up our spiritual hammers and begin your restoration.

America's
Self-Respect Crisis

Look around the malls, restaurants, sidewalks, and television shows of America, and you will see the many signs of a society in the throes of a self-respect crisis. Couples go on *The Jerry Springer Show* and embarrass each other for nothing more than fifteen minutes of fame. Dangerously overweight people stuff in one more ice cream cone, caring little about what they are doing to their body or the poor example they are setting for others. Perfectly normal, attractive women seem to go out of their way to make themselves come across looking as poorly as possible.

I frequently do book signings where I sit at a table in a bookstore, greet people who have purchased one of my books, and sign it for them. I am amazed at the difference in the way people take care of themselves. Some are in very good condition, while others look like they are ready to expire. Some have soft skin while others resemble an alligator. Some are well-groomed, others totally unkempt. I don't believe this difference is the result of one person having a terrible life while another has a fairy-tale existence. These people are making choices about how they present themselves to the world.

It's true that you can't judge a book by its cover, but that is usually what makes you pick it up! Like it or not, what we see does affect us, and we begin to form opinions based on it. I always tell the employees who answer the ministry telephones that they are the first person who gives an impression of Joyce Meyer Ministries, and that first impression is very important. Scripture teaches us not to judge by appearance or too hastily, which I agree with, but that does not alter the fact that how we present ourselves affects the way people think about us. And if we know this, why do some people choose to present such a terrible first impression?

The underlying factor is self-respect, or lack thereof. When we have something we believe is valuable, we make an effort to take care of it.

I assure you that this is not a matter of style. It's not simply that a grungier style is "in" now, and that these people are actually making a good impression on their peers. I admit, in my day you were expected to dress up whenever you went out, and it took me some time to get used to today's casual style. But I can tell the difference between somebody who does a good job of styling themselves casually and someone who is simply sloppy and does nothing to take care of themselves. I don't form opinions based on style. But if people look sickly or unclean, if they look a lot older than they really are, then I have concern for them.

I know a woman who was verbally abused by an alcoholic father. He repeatedly told her she was no good and accused her of immoral things of which she was not guilty. This treatment caused her to grow up feeling as if she had no value. She wasn't treated as valuable, so she did not value herself. Neither did she take care of herself. She actually could have been a very attractive woman, but she did virtually nothing with her qualities. She had long, dark, thick, beautiful hair, but she left it hanging in her face as if she was hiding from something. Her daily outfit was worn-out jeans, a baggy shirt, and dirty tennis shoes. She did not take care of her skin, so it was rough and dry. She was depressed, had a serious case of arthritis, stomach problems, hormone problems, nerve problems, and a variety of other aches and pains. She rarely ever bought herself anything because deep down she didn't feel she deserved it. Even when I gave her gifts to make her feel loved and valuable, she had a difficult time receiving them because of the way she felt about herself.

Have you known people like this? They're more common than we like to admit, aren't they? I saw in this woman, as well as many others I have encountered, what I believe to be a connection between low self-esteem and an unwillingness to make any investment in taking care of oneself. The two are closely related, and the arrow can go both ways. People with good self-esteem are more likely to take care of themselves, and people who take the time to do the little things to make themselves look and feel good are more likely to hold a positive self-image. More likely to make better parents. More loving partners. Quality workers. Smarter entrepreneurs.

Look great, feel great. Feel great, look great. It's no coincidence that the two often go together. If I have a day when I don't feel good physically but I go ahead and put on a nice comfortable outfit and fix my hair and face as usual, it always makes me feel better. It may not make me well, but it does make me feel better about myself in general.

My parents and my aunt live in an assisted-living complex. Many of the residents are eighty years old or older. It amuses and blesses me to see these elderly folks getting all dressed up to go to the dining room for dinner. (The facility actually has dress codes and the residents cannot even go into the halls in hair rollers and housecoats.) Some of the ladies wear lots of makeup and big jewelry as well as fancy dresses. The men often put on suits and ties. They head for the elevators around four in the afternoon, many of them pushing walkers but looking their best! I believe all of this helps these residents feel great about themselves. By looking the best they can, they feel younger and better.

The Wisdom of Investing in Your Health

I hope to reach many different types of people with this book. One group is the people who have given up on themselves, who consider themselves so little that they've stopped caring if they are tired, overweight, or sick, or if life passes them by without them ever enjoying it. In fact, some of them have given up on everything! They think it is easier not to expect anything good than to expect and be disappointed once again.

In truth, things aren't easier when you give up, because you then have to spend the rest of your life feeling like a failure and making excuses to God for why you aren't using the gift He's given you. What if your mother gives you a beautiful painting but you never get around to framing it? Every time she comes over, you feel guilty, bad, and lazy. You make another excuse, but deep down you know the truth is that you just did not care enough to do it. Well, guess what? God's coming around *every day*. He knows and sees everything, so it is time to stop making excuses and start making the most of the life God has given you.

Taking care of your life is not an indulgence. It's a way of respecting God and respecting other people, because when you don't care for yourself, when you end up sick and incapacitated, you let the burden of taking care of you fall to your family and society. When we feel bad we usually talk about it a lot, and even that can get burdensome for those around us. It is especially frustrating if they know we could make positive changes to help ourselves but we won't do it.

Then there is another, very different group I hope to reach. These folks certainly won't let life pass them by, but they get caught in a trap of their own. These are the Type A personalities, the overachievers who like themselves just fine and would say that they care about their health but have big, important things to do and can't be bothered by little things like exercise, diet, or self-care. If you're one of those people, I hope to convince you that you aren't doing the proper math. Rather than thinking of the time taken as wasted, you need to start thinking of it as an investment in your health—now, and especially for the future.

People have no problem investing in 401Ks or IRAs. Even though it takes money out of their pockets today, they know that, thanks to compounding interest, it will come back to them tenfold when they retire. Yet these same people are often unwilling to make the simple investments in their health and well-being that will ensure a happy future more than any 401K. And they don't even have to wait until retirement to claim it.

Investments you make in your health start paying off immediately, and they keep paying off for your entire life. What a deal! It's time you worried less about investing in stocks, bonds, or real estate, and worried a little more about *investing in yourself.*

Think about your car. You know it pays to do the little things like change the oil and the filters, rotate the tires, check the fluids and so on. You don't get any immediate benefit from doing these things, but you know what happens if you *don't.* Suddenly, the car doesn't work right and can't get you where you need to go. And destroying an engine block by running out of oil is *much* more expensive than simply putting in fresh oil every 3,000 miles.

I've heard my husband say, "They bought that car and never did any maintenance. They just ran it into the ground." Similarly, your body is your vehicle for getting you where you need to go in life. Not only physically, but spiritually, too. Don't refuse to do maintenance and run your body into the ground (the grave) earlier than God intended. Some people wait until they are ill to make an attempt to restore their health, but it is much easier on your body—and cheaper too!—to simply prevent yourself from getting sick in the first place. You don't wait to get a brake job until you crash into the car in front of you, and you shouldn't wait for your first stroke to start exercising. Flossing now is better than gum surgery later, a slower schedule now is better than a nervous breakdown later, and I know you'd rather stop eating three donuts and two candy bars daily now than face diabetes, insulin injections, and a dialysis machine in ten years.

Like any other kind of investment, investing in yourself now demands a little of your resources. In terms of money, it demands very little. Good food can be expensive, but you'll find that if you follow the guidelines in this book, and eat more whole foods and less processed food, you can actually save money. Drinking more water is free, as is walking and most other forms of exercise. Because many of the recommendations in this book involve less of something—eating less junk food, drinking fewer soft drinks, smoking less or not at all—you'll find that following God's plan leaves you with more money in your pocket each week.

The larger investment you need to make is one of time. First, you need to commit some time to learn how different foods affect your health and energy and how various lifestyles impact your stress level and mental well-being. We're not talking a huge commitment here—about as long as it takes you to read this book. A half-hour a day of exercise is a half-hour, true, but if it means a high-energy afternoon with many accomplishments, it may produce free time after all. Getting an extra hour of sleep counts as time used up only if you consider clutching your coffee cup like it's a life-preserver for an hour each morning as time well spent.

Whatever you do to invest in yourself now, know that it will pay off big time down the road. You'll avoid time spent in the hospital, or waiting in a doctor's office. You'll save money you would have spent on prescription drugs, sleeping pills, or therapists. Good health is cheap. Being sick is expensive.

Those things are easy to "put a price on." But, of course, the biggest return on your self-investment is priceless. It's your spirit. Every time you sell yourself short, you oppress your spirit. Every time you treat yourself right, that spirit soars a little higher.

Looking Nice Is Not a Sin

"Does God really care what I look like? Do I have to be thin?" More than one person has asked themselves this question in one way or another. The answer is that of course God doesn't judge us based on our looks, thankfully He sees our heart. But He does want us to look the best we can for His glory and honor. We represent Him and should always live with excellence in every area. Excellence simply means to take what you have and do the most you can with it. God does care what you feel like inside, and ultimately looking your best is simply a reflection of a healthy, happy-spirited internal state. I'm not talking *Cosmopolitan* cover-model good looks; the layers of touch-ups and fakery on those covers would astonish you. I'm talking the kind of normal, healthy appearance that makes people respond positively to you and that helps you feel the best you can about yourself.

Many Christians misunderstand the Bible's message to value inner beauty over outer appearance. They take the concept to an extreme, believing that any effort to look nice is a sin. What the apostle Peter says is:

Let not yours be the external adorning with interweaving and knotting of the hair, the wearing of jewelry, or changes of clothes; But let it be the inward adorning and beauty of the hidden person of the heart, with the incorruptible and unfading charm of a gentle and peaceful spirit, which is very precious in the sight of God.

I Peter 3:3–4

What Peter means is that you shouldn't confuse outer beauty for what is most important, which is a gentle and peaceful spirit. Don't be vain or put all your confidence in how you look. But Peter also doesn't say that the only way to be virtuous is to wear a brown sack, stop bathing, and give away all your possessions! True, a few people have found God by renouncing all material possessions, but in general I think it is much harder to find *anything* if you suffer the constant distractions of discomfort, or if you go out of your way to be as unattractive as possible and get mistreated by others because they think you are a religious fanatic. God cares most that you go forth clothed in righteousness. But righteousness *plus* a nice outfit never hurt anyone. If people see that you respect yourself, they'll respect you, too.

Like everything else in life, it is a question of balance. Keep the big picture in mind. Ask yourself, "What is the work that God has put me on earth to do?" Then decide what amount of attention you should pay to how you look and feel to get the maximum energy, health, and charisma you need to do that work as successfully as possible.

Using the 12-Key Plan
for Great Health

Rome was not built in a day, and neither was self-esteem. Personal health is an ongoing project. But like any big project, you begin with a solid foundation and build from there, and that's just what you're going to do in this book. Each of the next twelve chapters discusses one key to building a lifestyle that nurtures a sound spirit, soul, and body. Your task is to read each chapter, decide if you need to improve that area of your life or not, and if so, decide how to do it.

In each chapter, I'll explain what the key is and why it's so important to physical and spiritual success. I'll tell you how it's helped me or others. And then I'll give you five practical, down-to-earth suggestions for incorporating that change into your life. I don't expect you to take me up on all five; in fact, you don't have to take me up on *any* if you've got a better idea. Each chapter ends with a section called "Taking Action," where you get to write down one way—just one—that you will begin implementing that key.

What could be simpler? For example, for Key 7: Mindful Eating, all you would need to do is start saying grace before each meal. Or stop eating while you're doing other things. Or come up with your own small way to really be aware of what you are eating, rather than just eating without giving any thought to it. The success rate for complicated diets or challenging life-style changes is very low. I'd rather you choose one small thing and really commit to sticking with it than try to make many changes and lose hope after a few weeks. Besides, you may well find that once you make one change and realize how much better it makes you feel, you'll naturally want to make more.

But I'm not asking for that. I just want you to pick one behavior change, write it down—which makes you much more likely to take it seriously—and make it second nature before moving on to the next key. In the back of this book is a page for you to keep track of your twelve choices, to help remind yourself. Eventually, you'll have twelve small lifestyle changes you've adopted. That's a lot, considering how difficult it is to break old habits. If you really internalize these twelve little habits, you'll truly have changed, top to bottom, inside and out.

How Long Do I Spend on Each Key?

The amount of time you spend on each key is entirely up to you. The important thing is that you put in the necessary effort to succeed at each. Don't read Key 4: Exercise, decide to walk a half-hour each day, do it for three days, and then blow it off so you can get to Key 5: Balanced Eating. Make that half-hour walk your daily task for long enough that when you finally decide to start working on the next key, you automatically keep doing the walk each day.

So how much time is right? Certainly tackling a new key

each day would be too fast. A new key each month isn't necessarily too slow; that means you're taking the next year to commit yourself to physical and spiritual health, and it gives you plenty of time to work on each key before considering the next. I suggest you read the entire book so you have an idea of what you are working toward and then go back and take each key one at a time, putting the right amount of effort into one before going to another.

For most people, two to four weeks per key is probably about right. It all depends on how quickly you adapt to change, and how eager you are to get on with your new life. Be honest with yourself and you'll know what's right for you. I would prefer you take more time and achieve success in the end, than rush from one key to the next and within a few months not be doing any of them.

Why Twelve?

Twelve is a sacred number, a symbol of wholeness. Think of the twelve months of the year, of twelve hours of day and twelve of night. There were twelve tribes of Israel. And, of course, there were twelve apostles.

The twelve keys represent the fullness of life. By focusing on each one, you ensure balance. There won't be any corners of your life where illness—physical or otherwise—is allowed to fester. All it takes to *look great* and *feel great* is finding a little time to make friends with each one.

Each of the twelve keys has a specific focus, but all of them overlap. Just like the various pieces of your life and parts of your body, they are interconnected and reinforce each other. For example, getting more exercise (Key 4) is one of the best ways to reduce stress (Key 9). Reducing stress will help you curb your spiritual hunger (Key 8), which is essential for developing a healthy relationship with your body (Key 2), which will help you to create a positive vision of your future (Key 10). Healthy behaviors encourage other healthy behaviors, so you will probably find that as you go along, implementing each key in your life, it gets easier and easier, because you already have so many supports in place. Eventually, you'll create an incredible cathedral dome of vitality that seems to float effortlessly on its twelve columns of support.

Getting Started

You don't have to do the keys in the order listed, but it's probably a good idea. They build on each other, and the first few (right relationship with God, good self-esteem and healthy body image, and strong metabolism) provide the foundation for the rest.

As I mentioned previously, it's very important that you read all the keys before getting started. You'll want to think about future goals and about taking small steps to achieve large ones before starting off. It helps to have the big picture in place.

Got it? Now get going! Take your first step toward a new you!

Look Great
Feel Great

➤ KEY 1 ➤

Let God Do
the Heavy Lifting

If you can name a diet invented in the past forty years, chances are I've tried it. I've tried low-calorie, low-carb, and low-fat. I've tried liquid diets, hard-boiled egg diets, banana-and-milk diets, and the grapefruit diet. Some of these even worked at first. You know the routine. You embrace a new diet and you are fired up at how exciting this diet is. It's going to change your life! You tell all your friends about it! Your excitement gets you through the first couple of weeks and you lose a few pounds. Maybe you are really committed, you stick it out for a few months, and you drop ten or twenty pounds. But then you find it really inconvenient to stick to the diet. You eat out, or eat with friends, and none of your options quite fit the diet, so you make an exception. Then your schedule is so booked that you have to eat something on the run. Then the diet foods start to taste really boring, and you begin craving a little variety.

Pretty soon, the diet is gone. Slowly but surely you gain the weight back and sometimes more. I've gone through this countless times. Maybe you have, too. We think we're to blame. If only we weren't so weak, if we had more willpower, we'd be incredibly thin and healthy. Whether the goal in question is a weight-loss diet, an exercise routine, a change in how we treat other people, or any other self-improvement mission, failure makes us turn on ourselves. Soon we are wallowing in a pit of self-pity and disgust.

We criticize ourselves for our lack of willpower, but what if we don't fully understand the willpower principle? What if there is something we are leaving out that must come before willpower can ever be effective?

The Truth About Willpower

You know willpower. It's that thing that makes us dismiss the chocolate fudge sundae that's sitting in front of us, though every cell of our bodies screams for us to dig in. Willpower is that thing that CEOs and professional athletes tell us they use to trounce the competition. Willpower is what makes you get up and go jogging every morning.

Willpower sure sounds like a great thing. We are led to believe that we have enough of it to fight off every temptation that comes our way. And sometimes it works. But let me tell you a little secret about willpower. Willpower is your best friend when things go well, but it's the first friend to check out when you get weary. Willpower peers out Saturday morning at rain and forty-degree temperatures and says, "I'm staying home today!" The problem is that Willpower is closely aligned with Reason, and Reason is *always* open to being "reasoned" with and talked out of things. "You're right," it says, "too yucky out for jogging. Sure, you'll go twice tomorrow." Or: "Sure, finish the last piece of pie now so you don't have to put the plate back in the fridge, and then you'll eat a really small dinner tonight. Makes sense!" Reason is always willing to risk the slippery slope that leads to failure.

I have found that if I really don't want to do something, my mind gives me plenty of reasons why I don't have to. My emotion even joins in, saying, "I agree because I don't feel like doing it anyway." Our soul (mind, will, emotions) would love to run our lives, but the Bible says we are to be led by God's Spirit. We are never instructed to be willpower-led, we are told to be Spirit-led.

Willpower and discipline are important and vitally necessary to a successful life, but willpower alone won't be enough. Determination gets you started and keeps you going for awhile, but it is never enough to bring you across the finish line.

Not by might, nor by power, but by My Spirit says the Lord of hosts.

Zechariah 4:6 (NKJV)

Now, what happens if, instead of turning first to willpower in your time of need, you turn to God instead? God releases His power into your willpower and energizes it to bring you across the finish line. Willpower does not get the credit for our success, God does. Jesus said in John 15:5, "Apart from Me you can do nothing." This is one of the most important and most difficult lessons we must learn if we want to enjoy the life Jesus died to give us. When we go to anything or anyone before God, He is insulted and is obligated to let us fail so we will realize that "except the Lord builds the house, they labor in vain that build it" (Psalm 127:1).

We must learn to let God do the heavy lifting. Let Him supply the ability to energize our choices. We can choose to exercise or stop overeating, but our choice alone is not enough for complete victory. As I said previously, willpower and determination will get us started, but they've been known to quit in the middle and leave us stranded. God never quits in the middle.

There are some people in the world who claim to be a self-made success, but if we follow their lives all the way through, they usually end up falling apart. God has not created us to function well without Him, and the sooner we learn that the better off we will be.

Start by asking God to get involved, to do the heavy lifting. Continue on with God and finish with God. What should we do when the burdens in life seem too heavy? Jesus said, "Come to me."

> Come to me, all you who are weary and burdened, and I will give you rest.
>
> Matthew 11:28 (NIV)

Breaking Your Bonds

Whether your weakness is overeating, substance addiction, or simply well-worn patterns of poor personal maintenance, you are in bondage and unable to lead the life God intended for you until these things are dealt with. God has an awesome plan for you, but it requires you to learn the power you have as His child and begin exercising it. You can break out of old patterns that are destructive and start living the new and exciting life of freedom that God has for you. This is a terrific responsibility, and some people fear it. Freedom is our natural state, but if we haven't experienced it in a long time, it can be scary. We may instead prefer the ease of our familiar bonds. A prisoner who feels safe in his cell may stay in it, even when we fling open the door to his freedom. His prison cell might be dirty or confining, but it doesn't matter to him because he is accustomed to it and does not want to venture out into the unknown. His confining quarters are the only life he knows.

Like that prisoner, some people would rather endure the familiar tortures of diets, low energy, poor health, self-abuse, and exhaustion than taste freedom, because to be free they must learn to do things a completely different way. Change is difficult for many people. I have discovered that only one thing is more frightening than change, and that is the thought of never changing. Genuine and permanent change concerning the truth about why we are not taking care of ourselves may require some deep soul-searching, and not everyone is willing to do that. Only the truth sets us free (John 8:32) but truth is not always easy to face. In fact, facing the truth about ourselves is one of the bravest things we can ever do.

How many prisons of our own do we mistake for shelters? Many of us labor for years or even lifetimes under the burden of our bondage, believing that it is helping us and wondering why we never quite manage to succeed and move on. The diet is helping us lose those twenty pounds, even if we always slip back and start over. We may experience some temporary success using our old methods, but what we truly desire is permanent freedom. It is much better to be free from overeating than to live a lifetime of going on a diet, losing twenty pounds, gaining it back, and going through the same cycle again.

When you are discouraged about the condition your life or body is in, or struggling for the umpteenth time to lose weight, that first step seems like the heaviest one in the world. The burden of getting better, and the immensity of the journey before you, feels unbearable. A short-term diet may appear easier than a lifetime change, but it never brings freedom. Temporary relief is not freedom! I want you to be free!

Soul-searching, facing truth, and making necessary changes will be unbearable, so long as you try to "bear" it yourself. The bonds are too strong, the powers arrayed against you too formidable. Only God is strong enough to lift that burden. If you turn things over to God, the Source of Divine Strength, you will finally find the power you need to break free. Draw on the limitless power of the Holy Spirit, rather than your own very limited power. He will always lead you to victory and freedom.

> *If you turn things over to God, you will finally find the power you need to break free.*

But those who wait on the Lord shall renew their strength;
They shall mount up with wings like eagles, they shall run
and not be weary, they shall walk and not faint.

Isaiah 40:31 (NKJV)

Science Catches On

You don't have to take my word about God's ability to help you succeed. Even science is *finally* starting to come around to the fact that faith works. Study after study proves it. By monitoring people's physiological responses, scientists have learned that meditation and prayer lowers heart rate and blood pressure and improves the function of the immune system.

What about letting God help you with your goals? Well, compared to non-churchgoers, according to recent studies, those who attend church weekly are thirty-nine percent more successful at overcoming alcoholism and seventy-eight percent more successful at quitting smoking. They get fifty-four percent more exercise than non-churchgoers and are a whopping 131 percent less likely to be depressed! (And remember, this is after factors like socioeconomic level are taken into account. The only difference between these groups is their amount of faith.)

Knowing this, perhaps you won't be surprised at the biggest finding: the life expectancy of a non-churchgoer is seventy-five years, while weekly churchgoers live a healthy eighty-two years, and those who are involved more frequently live even longer. A large Duke University study of elderly adults found that those who engaged in prayer or Bible study at home were forty-seven percent less likely to die during the six years of the study than those who didn't.

Believe it or not, scientists can't figure out *why* those with faith do better, are healthier, and live longer than those without. While you and I smile and shake our heads, they pursue their little theories and studies like rats in a labyrinth, not seeing the Elephant in the middle of the room. They keep looking for answers when The Answer is right in front of them.

Five Ways to Trust God with Your Burdens

1. Ask

You will be amazed at what a huge difference it makes to directly invite God into your life to help solve your problems. It's astonishing how few people actually try this—even Christians! You need to take the time to quiet your mind and open it to God. Ask Him to be your partner in your personal restoration. Ask Him to forgive you for all the years you have ignored Him and tried to do things without His help. Open up this "God-space" in your soul and feel Him rush in to fill it with joy.

Even the most talented people in the world, with vast willpower, need this help. When Boston Red Sox pitcher Curt Schilling woke up the morning of his 2004 World Series start, his ankle was in such pain that he was sure he wouldn't be able to pitch. So, said Schilling, "I went to the Lord for help, because I knew I wasn't going to be able to do this myself." Hardly able to walk, Schilling pitched one of the most brilliant games of his life.

2. Attend Church

Some people manage to maintain very special relationships with the Lord for years without any support. They are few and far between. Most of us find that the weekly boost of prayer, education, community, and sacred space we get at church gives us a far stronger bond. If you are struggling for ways to make contact with God, and you haven't tried church yet, what on earth are you waiting for?

3. Attend a Support Group

Support groups exist for a variety of problems, from alcohol to drug-addiction to overeating. They can help you admit you are powerless in the face of your bond and encourage you to turn your restoration over to God. If you work best when you can share your struggle with others who are going through the same thing, then I encourage you to seek out one of these groups. Even a group of trusted friends who meet once a week for coffee can be a big boost. Some people are more likely to exercise if they go to a class and do it with other people. If you need support from others, don't be afraid to ask for it.

4. Begin Each Day with an Affirmation

First thing when you wake up in the morning, before all the craziness of the day comes flying at you, take a moment to renew your vows to God and refresh your spirit with His strength. This will give you the mental and emotional peace that is the foundation of success. You can write an affirmation that addresses your specific needs, or you can use this one that I wrote:

"God, I am free by the power of Your Word. I believe You have given me the strength to break free from the bonds that have been holding me back from all the beautiful things You have planned for me. I thank You that I am free by the blood of Jesus and the sacrifice that He made on the cross of Calvary. Thank You for making me free through the truth of Your Word and for empowering me with Your power, strength, and wisdom. Help me to be all You want me to be. In Jesus' name, amen."

5. Pray in Moments of Doubt

No matter who you are, you will find moments when your determination weakens, when you are sorely tempted to blow off some action that is one of your keys to lifetime health. When you get that feeling, don't quit, but don't blindly bull forward with the activity, either. Step back, take a moment, and call on God to come to you and carry you through. Renew your strength in that moment of peace, and then journey forth with new passion, trust, and confidence.

 TAKING ACTION ➤➤➤

"Be doers of the Word, and not hearers only."
(James 1:22)

Choose at least one action you can take to have a closer walk with God and begin letting Him do the heavy lifting. Write it down, *commit to it,* and start today.

Action: _____

➤ KEY 2 ➤

Learning to
Love Your Body

What if everywhere you went, you ran into someone you didn't like? Wouldn't that be terrible? "Oh, no," you'd think, "*her* again." You attend a party and you have to endure her conversation and views. You go to church and she's sitting right beside you. "What a bummer to have to spend so much time with this person," you think. Then it gets worse. There she is at the dinner table with you! She's lounging by the pool, she's even in your bed! She's everywhere!

That sounds pretty awful, but it is the exact situation you find yourself in if you don't like yourself, because you are everywhere you go. You can't get away from yourself, even for a second, so you are in for a sad life if you dread your own company.

That much is pretty obvious. But believe it or not, even though we can all agree that it makes no sense to live your life this way, I find that *most* people don't like themselves. They may not even realize it, but some genuine soul-searching reveals the sad fact that they have rejected themselves and in some cases even hate themselves. I've come across a lot of people over the years, through my ministry and in day-to-day life, and I'm amazed at how few are truly at peace with themselves. Instead, they have declared war on themselves, and the cause, quite frequently, is the body.

How can so many of us hate our bodies, our faithful servants which are only there to help us be all God wants us to be while we're on Earth? I can think of a number of factors, all of which I have at least a passing familiarity with.

1. *Abuse in childhood.* We are all born with a loving attitude toward our bodies. Small children instinctively enjoy their bodies; they care for them and protect them. They never think about what their bodies look like until they are older. But this natural understanding that the body is good flips by negative messages or mistreatment. I know this firsthand. The physical and emotional abuse I suffered as a child told me loud and clear that my body was bad and that I was worthless. When the only physical experiences you have are of pain and discomfort, you learn to hate your body as the source of those feelings. You wish it didn't exist. Sometimes you even want to punish your body for the bad things "it" did to you. Because I was sexually abused, I saw my body as the source of my emotional pain. I thought often that if only I was not a girl, then the abuse wouldn't happen. As a teenager I was always "chubby." I was not extremely overweight, but enough to be teased and to feel even worse about my body than I already did.

Even when you grow up and the abuse stops, your disrespect and disgust for your body remains. And when you aren't living in harmony with your body, all sorts of bad situations develop. You don't exercise, because that's getting "too close" to your body. (Or you exercise excessively, as a way of shrinking your body and making it disappear.) You don't want to support your body with good food, and this can lead to eating disorders such as anorexia (self-starvation) or bulimia (binging and purging).

Some women who are sexually abused intentionally gain huge amounts of weight to make sure men won't find them attractive. They don't want to be desired for their body. Others just don't take care of themselves because they don't feel they are worth the effort. Poor examples are another problem. Your role models may have had internal problems that made it difficult to care for their own health, and you are merely doing what was modeled in front of you.

The abuse doesn't have to be sexual or physical to cause these problems. Authority figures or even peers are perfectly capable of driving home the message that we are bad or useless and that our bodies are ugly and evil. Until you confront your feelings and find peace, you will be in a constant state of warfare with yourself, and will experience the stress, trauma, and exhaustion that war always causes. God wants you to be at peace with yourself.

Anyone who has a root of shame about who they are in their life will be poisoned from the inside out. That poisoned root must be replaced with God's unconditional love and acceptance. We must learn to love ourselves in a balanced way and embrace who we are at this moment in time.

2. *Misunderstanding the Bible's teachings.* It's true that the Bible tells us to resist the flesh and embrace the spirit, but that doesn't mean hate the flesh! The flesh is weak, the spirit is strong, and so we need to use the spirit's strength to lovingly guide the flesh. Instead, however, too many people believe they would be fine if not for that awful flesh tempting and confusing them. They blame the body for interfering with their spiritual development, and wish they could just get rid of it. They forget that the body is the temple for the Holy Spirit. The people in the world cannot see my spirit. All they see is my body, so if I am to spread God's love, I'd better use my body to do it! My hands need to be the hands of Jesus; my feet, His feet; and my mouth, His mouth. Romans 12:1 teaches us to offer all of our faculties as a living sacrifice for God's use. Don't hate your body, but use it to bring glory to God!

3. *Media messages.* Do you resemble the models you see in magazines and billboards, or the actresses in TV and movies? Neither do I! They are stunningly beautiful, impossibly thin, and suspiciously tall. Their hair, teeth, and skin are perfect. It's impossible to try and compete with that. But I'm pleased to say that I've reached a stage in my life where I no longer expect to, and don't even wish to. I've learned that kind of beauty often owes itself to a lot of help from outside sources. To get the models to look as they do on magazine covers, a lot of "tricks of the trade" are used. Tricks like lighting, makeup, and computer airbrushing are all necessary to create the illusions we see everyday—illusions of flawless people that have zero connection to real life. Twenty-five years ago, the average fashion model weighed eight percent less than the average woman (and was a bit taller). Today, at 5'10" and 114 pounds, the average model is six inches taller than the average woman but weighs twenty-five percent less. Don't spend your life competing with an illusion! Don't live in the agony of unrealistic expectations!

Even if we know these things in our heads, the insidious

message still creeps into our subconscious that we are supposed to look like these models and actresses, rather than the thousands of regular people we see every day. And considering the unbridgeable gulf between how the models look compared to our appearances, it seems pointless to even try. We feel like giving up. Why work out when I'll never be 5'10" and 120 pounds? Bring on the Häagen-Dazs! Have you noticed that characters on TV wake up in the morning with all their makeup on, looking better than most of us do when we go out for an evening? They are not like the woman I heard of whose fiancé had never seen her without her makeup. The morning after their wedding night he awoke and was appalled to find her face on the pillow and someone rather frightening staring at him.

I manage to look fairly good by the time I go out, but I can promise you that I don't wake up looking "camera-ready." I have to work on it and so do other people. The good news is that I am willing and pleased to take what I have and do the best I can with it.

The media isn't trying to make us feel bad. They know all people are drawn to beauty, so they try to sell their products by showing us as much beauty as possible, even if it's a fake beauty. The real culprit who makes us feel bad is ego, the part of ourselves that finds meaning by seeing how we stack up against other people. Ego is the opposite of spirit, because it doesn't look internally at all. If we have a bigger house, better legs, or more successful children than the people around us, then ego feels pretty good. Ego likes it if we are smarter than other people. The problem with ego, though, is that there is always somebody out there smarter, richer, or prettier than we are—especially when we compare ourselves not just to the people in our neighborhood but to the ones on TV, too. So ego can always find something to feel bad about. Ego is never satisfied.

Christ's teachings are the best I know for learning to ignore ego (the flesh) and embrace spirit. They are what did it for me. As it says in 1 Corinthians 1:27–29 (NIV):

"God chose the foolish things of the world to shame the wise; God chose the weak things of the world to shame the strong. He chose the lowly things of this world and the despised things—and the things that are not—to nullify the things that are, so that no one may boast before him."

God chooses what the world throws away as useless. There are no hopeless cases, no useless people in God's eyes. Each of us is His special creation. We are not an accident and if we will give Him the opportunity, He will restore everything that has been damaged and help us be someone that even we can be delighted to be.

Ego thrives on competition and striving to be first, but what is the point of competition? What does it get you? Not contentment. Not joy. It can't get you the one thing that matters— eternal salvation and peace with God. To get that, you have to forsake ego and embrace spirit, and often the ones who have the easiest time doing this are not the powerful or the rich, but the meek. These are the ones who know they are nothing without God and have no problem with it. They are the ones God has chosen to work through. Instead of competition, spirit thrives on cooperation and love, because the only true goal is to know God, and then to help others, through love, to do the same.

I'm at peace with my body. I love it. I support it, and it supports me. I don't feel any need to look like a model. Models often find their beauty to be more of a burden than a blessing anyway, because they must live in constant fear of losing it. I'm sixty-three, and simply expect my body to reflect what I am: a healthy, happy, sixty-three-year-old woman. I strongly believe in taking what we have to work with and doing the most we can with it. I try to look my best but I don't allow myself to be pressured by unrealistic expectations.

4. The Beauty Industry. The beauty industry can be even more dangerous to us than the media if we don't like ourselves. The media makes you feel bad by showing you extraordinarily beautiful people. The beauty industry—which includes beauty-care products, weight-loss products, and diet foods—needs to make you feel that you cannot be what you should be without their product. Although some of the products are excellent and may help us, we cannot allow ourselves to be deceived by thinking that all we need is one more cream, today's most popular diet, or a pill that promises we will be able to eat everything we want to and still lose weight overnight while we sleep. Don't fall into the trap of thinking that by following the beauty industry's advice, you will be beautiful.

The truth is that you are already beautiful in God's eyes and if you will accept yourself and follow God's principles, you will systematically look better on the outside. I look better today than I did twenty years ago. I worry less and I am happier; therefore, I look more refreshed.

God loves you. He wants you to receive His love and accept

yourself. Take better care of yourself beginning today. If you have a good relationship with God and know your value, you will not be desperate for the newest beauty cream, pill, or program.

If you genuinely feel that a program or product will help you, then go for it, but don't desperately try everything that exists, only to experience failure after failure that results in you feeling worse about yourself than when you started.

What about cosmetic surgery? It's becoming more and more popular and even affordable. Is it right or wrong? If we have cosmetic surgery does it mean we have a poor self-image? Does it mean we are vain? Should we be satisfied with ourselves the way we are? Let me begin by saying I have had some procedures done on my face and I did not do it because I was insecure. My work in spreading God's Word requires that I be on television. To feel confident in doing so, I need to look my best. I prayed about it for a long time and felt God gave me a release to do it if I really wanted to.

I don't believe people should get out of balance and think cosmetic surgery can solve all their problems. No matter how many facelifts or liposuctions you have, you are still you; if you don't like who you are, you won't feel any better than you did before the procedure. However, I don't think it is wrong to do what you can to help yourself. If people have crooked teeth, they do not hesitate to have them fixed. I know a woman who had large bags under her eyes and severely drooping eyelids. After cosmetic surgery, she looked ten years younger and much more refreshed and happy. I recommend that you pray about everything and don't do anything unless you know your motives are right and you have peace about doing it.

5. *Age and Sickness.* You can grow up in a loving and supportive environment, be comfortable with your looks and immune to the spells of the beauty industry, and still fall out of love with your body as you age. Your activity level slows down, your metabolism slows, you put on a few pounds, you notice creaks in your joints, and suddenly everybody seems younger, faster, and thinner than you. It's worse if you have a job and lifestyle that doesn't encourage exercise. You start to resent your body and its limits.

If you don't want to start hating your body, you need to stay active, which I'll discuss in Key 4: Exercise, but you also need to develop a realistic picture of what you should feel and look like at that stage of life. Fifty-year-olds shouldn't try to look like twenty-year-olds, nor necessarily expect to feel like them. Age does make a difference. I can actually say that I feel better now than I did twenty years ago, because I have learned how to take care of myself, but I must be honest and also say that I don't have the stamina I did twenty years ago.

My husband Dave is very healthy, has exercised most of his life, has a strong heart, and feels good almost all the time. Three years ago he still went twice a year for a special golf outing with his friends to play fifty-four holes of golf a day for four days straight. Two years ago, he noticed that it took longer to recover from those outings and he finally decided that due to his age he shouldn't play more than thirty-six holes a day during the four days. Dave is sixty-six years old; playing thirty-six holes of golf a day for four days in hot weather is outstanding! Yet even he cannot do everything he once could.

I used to weigh 135 pounds, and then at some point in my late-fifties I gained six pounds and have been that way ever since. My metabolism slowed down and those six pounds stuck. I'm not thrilled about it, but I accept it. I would have to seriously deprive myself to lose those six pounds and keep them off. My body and health seem very good where I am, so I have decided that I would rather live with my six pounds than never eat the things I enjoy. My body is also shaped so that I wear a size eight top and a size ten bottom. I have always been that way. There are lots of beautiful suits I can't buy because they don't come in split sizes. I could buy two suits and take what I needed, but then I'd feel like I had to find someone who was a size eight bottom and a size ten top, so I wasn't being wasteful! The whole situation used to frustrate me until I decided "It is what it is!" Now I mostly laugh about it—and laughing is a very important habit to have, especially as you age.

If your feet are larger than you would like them to be, or your body is not proportioned perfectly, or you are shorter than you wish you were, don't ever let it frustrate you again. Decide right now, "It is what it is!" I am going to be happy with what I have got and do the best I can with it.

These are some of the main factors that cause us to fall out of love with our bodies, and they can be pretty tough to ignore. But that doesn't mean I'm letting you off the hook! Not for one second. It's absolutely essential to your long-term physical and spiritual health that you overcome any unhealthy attitudes you may have about your body or yourself. And if you don't already have the tools to do so, you will by the end of this book.

> *Never forget that God wants you to love your body and yourself.*

Never forget that God wants you to love your body and yourself. He *expects* it, no matter what messages the world has given you. As the Bible says, "Do not conform any longer to the pattern of this world, but be transformed by the renewing of your mind" (Romans 12:2, NIV). Think about yourself in a new way. Determine to be the best "you" that you can, and stop trying to be what the world says you should be.

The world can tell you lots of things. It whispers untruths in your ear, many of them cruel. It also changes its views and fashions by the month. If you start following its lead, you are lost. Your friendship with yourself will be lost. But if, instead, you see yourself as God sees you, then not only will you love yourself, but you will have the confidence and faith to be a powerful force for good in the world.

Five Ways to Nurture Self-Love

1. Don't Chase Your Youth

As I've said, at sixty-three I feel really great—which shows that things like energy, health, and happiness don't need to decline as we age—but part of my contentment comes because I've become comfortable with who I am. I've succeeded at being myself. I don't pine away for my twenties, partly because I didn't like my twenties anyway, and partly because it wouldn't matter if I did! Here I am now, and I have chosen to live today!

People who long for their youth are never content, because every day that youth gets a little farther away. Don't despise getting old, because if you stay alive you can't avoid it. It's much better to enjoy who you are now and try to live and look appropriate for someone like you. It helps to find role models. We don't think of fifty- or sixty-year-olds as needing role models, but they do! Everyone does.

Think of some of the people in the world you most admire. Make a list. How many twenty-something-year-old actresses are on that list? Not many, I suspect. So why would you stress over trying to keep up with them, to look like them? You will be much happier and more effective if you model yourself on the people whose lives you truly want to emulate. Billy Graham is a good role model for me, and I can honestly say that I have never worried about how much he weighs or how many wrinkles he has. I admire him for his spirit, commitment, accomplishments, and dedication to God and his life's calling.

Celebrate Differences! I have a friend who eats as much as I do and weighs ninety-three pounds. I have another friend who eats less than me and weighs more. We are all different. Different ages, different metabolisms, different bone structures. Rather than resent that I don't have someone else's bone structure, I made a decision to enjoy the fact that we're all unique, and that my friend can eat like a horse and stay rail-thin. How boring it would be if everyone looked just like me.

In some cultures, such as Africa and Tibet, old age isn't dreaded, it's eagerly anticipated. People look forward to the time when all the busyness of life—school and career and child rearing and home buying—is behind them, and they can concentrate on the important stuff: spiritual growth, and enjoying life and family. Discontentment is one of the big giants we must conquer if we ever hope to enjoy life fully. Discontentment with looks, age, position, possessions, and anything else that makes us ungrateful for what we currently have. We may not have all we would like to have, but we certainly have more than some people. No matter how you think you look, there is somebody who would love to look like you. No matter how old you are, there is someone older who would love to be as young as you. Cheer up and make the best of things. Love yourself and love your life; it is the only one you have!

2. *Learn to Receive God's Love*

Nothing frustrates me more than people who don't know how to accept gifts. It's a joy to express my love or appreciation to someone by giving them a gift I know they'll like. But if the response is "No, no, I can't accept that," or "Really, you shouldn't have," or "No, take it back," then that drains all the joy out of it. It becomes downright embarrassing if you have to force a gift on someone. You may even wonder if you should have offered the gift at all.

Receiving a gift graciously stems from inner security. Those who are uncomfortable getting gifts usually have some deep-seated insecurity that prevents them from accepting others' kindness. They feel so low that they can't imagine they deserve anything. Or they worry that the gift burdens them with reciprocation. They would rather reject the gesture than have to engage in a relationship.

In my life and work I have opportunities to give many gifts, and I also get some. When I do, I genuinely appreciate it and tell people so. Be a giver and expect God to bless you through others. When they do, say "thank you" and graciously receive their offer.

The greatest gift that can be given is offered to each of us every day, yet few of us have the faith and self-esteem to accept it. God offers us His love. All we have to do is open our hearts and make the decision to receive it. Then we in turn get to pass it on to others. Receiving God's love is an important step because we can't love others without it. We cannot give away what we do not have.

You see, receiving is an action. It isn't passive. You must make the decision to reach out and grab it. Think of a wide receiver catching a pass in football. He isn't called the *wide target*. He doesn't just stand there and wait for the quarterback to stick the ball in his hand. No, he *wants* that ball. He goes after it like a dog after a bone. He'll do anything to get it.

That's how you need to receive God's love. Be passionate about it. Go after it. Study God's love. Meditate on it. As you seek it eagerly, you will receive a revelation deep in your heart that will change your life.

For years I desperately wanted to be a good Christian, to give my love to others and have them love me back to help fill the emptiness I felt inside. Yet it never quite worked. I couldn't understand why, and I became frustrated with myself and others. Why was I unable to walk in love? Why weren't people giving me the love I needed? Then I finally realized that I had never received God's love—I'd never reached for it. I never liked myself; I felt unworthy of any gift, and certainly of one as immense as God's love! I made the commitment, opened my heart, and let God rush in with His healing love. Then and only then was I able to love myself, to walk in and enjoy His perfect love, to give my love to others, and feel their love come back to me tenfold.

3. Focus on the Journey, Not the Destination

You know the routine. You pack the kids into the minivan for the long trip to Grandma's or Disney World, and five minutes out of the driveway it starts: "Are we there yet?" I can remember as a kid feeling like it took *forever* to get anywhere; I was so excited about the destination that the hours of driving were torture. As an adult I continued the same wrong attitude and spent a lot of miserable years never enjoying where I was because I was too focused on my destination. I finally learned that life is about the journey, not the destination, and then the ride became much more fun. Time does not go by any faster if we are frustrated about it, so we should learn to "wait well."

On your own journey toward looking great and feeling great, you also need to enjoy the ride. What matters is not where you are, or how far away your destination is, but the direction you are headed. If you live in New York and are headed for Disney World in Florida, you've got a long way to go, but you will get there, no question, as long as you keep heading south. On the other hand, somebody else can be in Orlando, a lot closer to Disney than you, but if she heads north, she will never get there. Be excited that you are headed in the right direction. Even reading this book is a step in the right direction, so go ahead and feel good about it.

The important thing is not what you weigh today, or how far you can run, but that you are improving. If your goal is to lose fifty pounds and you lose two pounds the first week, should you get discouraged because you are forty-eight pounds heavier than you want to be? No. You say, "Hallelujah, what a great week!" and continue with your plan.

Be proud of *today*. Don't go beyond that. Don't look at how far you have to go, look at how far you have come. As Jesus said, "Do not worry about tomorrow, for tomorrow will worry about itself. Each day has enough trouble of its own" (Matthew 6:34, NIV). Do everything you can to make the day a success, and when it is, allow yourself some deep satisfaction in the evening.

Think about your successes rather than your failures. Maybe you ate a little too much today, but the good news is you didn't eat as much as you used to before beginning your new journey toward lifetime health and wholeness. Perhaps you intended to walk thirty minutes but got started late and could only do twenty minutes. Don't feel that you are a failure and should have done better; remember when you did not exercise at all and be happy for your progress. Keeping this positive attitude about your progress will breed more progress.

Let your days be filled with good choices, healthy food, lots of activity, and good thoughts. Then your body and soul will be healthy, fit, and virtuous. Don't focus on your body, focus on the day. Have one good day, and tomorrow becomes more enjoyable, and leads to an even better day. As you enjoy the journey, you'll soon discover just how easy it is to love and affirm yourself.

4. Learn the Facts

Chances are, you're a lot closer to average than you think. Here's some information to help you understand that not everyone is rail-thin with three percent body fat.

The average woman in America is 5'4" and weighs 152 pounds. She wears a size twelve. Surprised? Then join the Distorted Image club. I always encourage people to be excellent, not average. But looking at the norm can help us realize that our condition isn't as bad as we thought. In America we seem obsessed with weight, yet fitness should be more important to us than pounds. There are many skinny people who are in very poor condition physically, mentally, emotionally, and spiritually. If I had a choice of being ten pounds overweight, healthy and happy, or ten pounds underweight, miserable and unhealthy, I would choose the extra pounds. I already told you that I weigh six pounds more than I used to and six pounds more than I want to, but I refuse to be obsessed with it. You may think that six pounds is not even worth mentioning, but each person's situation is important to them. If I let it, my six pounds could bother me just as much as someone else's fifty pounds.

I am not suggesting that we can be overweight and just not care. But I am suggesting that we be more health-conscious than weight-conscious. I firmly believe that if we concentrate on good health we will ultimately weigh what is right for us as individuals.

A study at the Cooper Institute for Aerobics Research in Dallas tracked 22,000 men for eight years and found that risk of death was connected to fitness, not weight. Fit men who were slightly overweight were no more likely to die than fit men of normal weight, and unfit men of normal weight had the same risk of death as unfit men who were overweight. The reason we've been confused for years on this issue is because fit people often have normal weights, but the benefits—health, long life, high energy—come from the fitness, not the weight.

We live in an age where thin is in, and where our attitudes toward fat run close to hysteria. Lose weight if you feel you need to, but don't let anyone tell you that your weight is unhealthy or unnatural if it isn't. And by all means don't let a few pounds keep you from loving and accepting yourself.

Remember, this isn't a license to ignore what you weigh, but it is an invitation to refrain from obsessing over it. Concentrate on being healthy and fit because it significantly decreases your risk of life-threatening health problems, makes you feel great, and reduces your risk of many diseases, as I'll discuss later.

I spent most of my life wanting to be skinny and never caring whether or not I was healthy. In the process I was neither skinny nor healthy. Since I learned to concentrate on health, my weight has stayed within a few pounds of a normal range.

This may be a new way for you to think, but I honestly believe it is important for your success. I know a woman who has spent most of her adult life battling her weight, and she recently told me that she was totally disgusted with having her weight on her mind every day. She said, "I want to be healthy and I believe if I am, then I will weigh what I am supposed to weigh." Good for her; she now has a mindset that will ultimately lead to victory.

5. View Your Body as a Friend

If your body is larger than you would like, with aches and pains you are tired of, don't treat it as an enemy. If you do, you will probably never see progress in the areas that you would like to improve. If you had a friend who was sick or in need, you would do everything you could to help them. That is exactly the attitude you should have toward your body. If it isn't what you want it to be, do everything you can to help it; don't despise it or fight it.

We blame our bodies for a lot of things they aren't responsible for. After all, our bodies are a product of what we have put into them and how we have treated them for years and years. I would not blame my automobile for falling apart if I put glue in the gas tank instead of gasoline. Perhaps we should apologize to our bodies for mistreating them. Whatever problems we have, the fault lies with us, not our bodies. We made poor choices that only we can reverse. Accept your body today as your friend and companion for life, and start developing a relationship with it that will be rewarding.

➤➤➤ TAKING ACTION ➤➤➤

"Be doers of the Word, and not hearers only."
(James 1:22)

Choose at least one action you can take to nurture self-love. Write it down, *commit to it,* and begin today.

Action: _____

➤ KEY 3 ➤
Mastering Metabolism

The Secret to Stable Weight

Have you ever wished you could own a masterpiece, like an original Van Gogh or Monet painting? You may think you could never afford such a masterpiece, but the truth is that you were born with one. The human body is God's own masterwork. Part of what makes it so special is its amazing versatility. You were made to survive in all kinds of situations, which is why your body is so adaptable. If you soak up a lot of sun, your body automatically creates extra pigment in your skin to protect you. If you use your muscles every day, your body starts making those muscles bigger to help you out. What a system!

One way in which your body constantly adapts is through *metabolism*. We hear this term all the time. If we see a skinny woman who is always energetic, or a man who eats like a horse but never gains a pound, we say that person has a high metabolism. People who are less energetic and gain weight easily often say they must have a slow metabolism. But what do we really mean by metabolism? And what impact does it have on our waistline and energy level?

Metabolism is simply the process by which your body breaks down, or *metabolizes* your food and converts it into energy. All our energy comes from the food we eat (despite what certain pills and supplements may claim). We literally burn the food to power ourselves, just as your car burns gasoline for power. But remember, the body is a masterwork, far more sophisticated than even the nicest Mercedes. We can burn all sorts of things for fuel, from a chicken to a potato to leaves of lettuce. And we can burn that fuel at very different rates, from extremely fast, hurtling down the highway in overdrive, to very slow, just barely inching forward in first gear.

That's the danger. When your metabolism feels sluggish, that means you are creeping along, stuck in first gear. You aren't burning much energy, which means you don't *have* much energy. That's not a fun place to be—for your body or your brain. You feel down, uninspired. You can't quite wake up, while others seem to zoom past you.

If you aren't using much energy but are still "filling up your tank" with as much food as usual, you are in trouble. If you kept putting more gas in your car than you used, the extra would just spill out the top of the tank. But remember, your body is way more sophisticated than your car. It has an incredibly flexible system for storing as much fuel as it can get. Millions of special, flexible cells throughout your body swell up with the extra fuel, saving it for later. It's as if your car had inflatable rubber tanks all over it that could fill up with unlimited amounts of gasoline.

Great system, right? Well, yes, but you might not think it's so great when I tell you the name of these cells: fat cells. Fat is an extremely efficient way of storing energy for later. Your body can convert any kind of food into fat, store the fat, and then convert the fat back into energy and use it when needed.

Don't blame the body. We live in a very unusual period in history, when food is abundant and most of us (at least in the developed world) have more than we need. But until the invention of modern farming techniques, modern factories, and modern vehicles to distribute the food, famine was a common situation. Our ancestors worried more often about hunger than what to do with a surplus. That may be one of the reasons why, when faced with a pile of spare ribs, we have a natural instinct to overeat. Sure, we don't need the extra fuel right now, but if we get as much as we can while it's in front of us, and store what we don't use as fat, that will come in really handy next time the crops fail and we have to live off that fat for a while. Millions of our ancestors were saved from famine by fat they stored in times of abundance.

The body has another survival trick up its sleeve. Not only does it store energy for lean times in the future, it also tries to be careful about the rate at which it uses these resources. You probably run your household the same way. If you get a promotion, you loosen up the purse strings a bit. Maybe you build an addition, or go on fancier vacations. You know more is coming in, so why not spend a little? On the other hand, if you lose your job, you immediately cut back on expenses to get by as long as possible on your savings. You hold off on new purchases, turn the heat down a little in winter, and travel less. Your body works the same way. If it doesn't get much food (or water), it assumes that hard times are here, and it does what it can to get you through. It says, "Whoa, let's slowwwwwww things down a little until some good food comes along." It turns off the lights, turns down the heat, and tries to travel as little as possible.

It slows your metabolism.

And you know what that feels like. You don't want to move. Your brain is groggy. You're cold all the time. You don't do much of anything. You just feel down. And you are burning very few calories, which is great if you are stranded on a desert island, but terrible if you are trying to lose weight.

Why Diets Backfire

You can see why diets wreck metabolism. Any diet that tries to achieve weight-loss by drastically cutting back on the number of calories you eat is doomed, because it's based on a misunderstanding of how the human body works. It seems logical enough: eat less, burn more, lose weight. And yes, that is the path to weight loss. The only way to lose weight is to burn more calories per day than we consume. When that happens, the body liquidates your fat reserves and burns them to make up the extra calories. You literally melt the fat right off your body!

But as I just explained, your body's natural instinct is not to keep reviving your metabolism once your food intake goes way down. Not long after you start dieting, it's going to lower your metabolism to match the new amount of food coming in. This explains the classic dieting dilemma most of us are all too familiar with:

You go on a diet and have great success the first few weeks. The pounds fall off and you think you've got it made. But then, even though you are sticking (with difficulty) to the diet and eating like a bird, suddenly the weight loss stops. You lose a couple of pounds one week, then one the next, then none.

I've seen this happen with my daughter. Years ago, Laura wanted to lose weight, so I designed a special calorie-restriction diet for her. She followed it to the letter. She lost a couple of pounds, then nothing! Her metabolism adjusted. I'd always thought people who didn't lose weight on diets must be cheating. Now I saw first-hand evidence that wasn't the case.

Diets don't just offer limited weight loss. You can also feel sluggish, depressed, and you crave "real food." Soon you start sneaking forbidden foods and slipping off the diet. And the weight comes back with a vengeance! You even seem to have more fat than before.

That's because your body is happy to add an extra pound of fat but refuses to give one up; those pounds go on easier than they come off. And when your metabolism is slow and you aren't doing much, you tend to lose muscle. The more you work a muscle, the bigger it gets, and the less you use it, the more it shrinks. Muscle looks great; it stays firm and flexes when you move, as opposed to fat, which has all the shape of a water balloon and doesn't do anything when you move except jiggle. More importantly, muscle burns calories all the time, just keeping itself ready for action. The more muscle you have, the more calories you burn, *even when sleeping*. This is your resting metabolism, and it's different for every person.

Eventually, if you keep eating regularly, your body catches up and starts increasing your metabolism. But your body has lost muscle so it's used fat to replace it. You may be the same weight as you started out, but you will look worse—because you have replaced firm muscle with fat—and you will burn fewer calories each day because you have less muscle and a lower resting metabolism. So you will find it more difficult than ever to maintain your weight.

For all these reasons, dieting is not the way to get to, or maintain, a healthy weight.

The good news is that there are plenty of things you can do to fix this situation! The key is to eat a normal, balanced diet and to engage in activities that keep your metabolism purring along at an energetic clip. Do this and you will gradually shed any excess pounds, until you are at a healthy weight. Remember, the goal is not just to be thin, but to be healthy and weigh what is right for you.

Five Ways to Boost Metabolism

1. Exercise

The most popular way to burn more calories is to *move*. As I'll explain in the next chapter, exercise causes your body to liquidate its fat reserves and send those molecules to your muscles to burn for energy. Just as your body interprets dieting as a food shortage and lowers metabolism to help out, it also assumes that if you move fast every day, you have a good reason; it must be key to your survival. So it raises metabolism, builds more muscle, and gives you the enzymes you need to burn calories more easily. The more regularly you exercise, the higher you keep your metabolism, and the more effortlessly those pounds will melt away. A fringe benefit of this is that you stay alert and happy more of the time.

2. Eat Breakfast (and Lunch and Dinner)

Cutting dessert out of your diet isn't going to send your body into a "no food!" panic. As long as you're getting three meals a day, even if the meals are a little smaller, your body will be content. Only when you skip a meal entirely does your body think, "Uh-oh, something weird is happening!" and begin to shut down.

We've all heard it said that breakfast is the most important meal of the day, and it turns out that's true. Think about it: you've fasted for nearly twelve hours. Your metabolism naturally slows down overnight, so breakfast is your body's signal to kick-start itself. A good breakfast gets the machinery working again. *All* the machinery: digestion, brain power, senses, muscle power. Because a good breakfast makes you so much more active, it can actually help you lose weight. Skipping breakfast just puts you in a state of lethargy; you creep through your morning, not getting much of anything accomplished— that includes burning calories.

I used to do that all the time. For years I was caught in the trap of not eating until mid-afternoon. I'd spend those days drinking coffee, smoking cigarettes, and in the evenings eating ravenously. And I wondered why I never lost weight and felt bad all the time! My metabolism crept through the day, and then got a big load of calories in the evening when I didn't need it.

If you are one of those people who gets queasy at the thought of breakfast, don't feel like you have to force down a three-course meal; even a little something will help get the engine started. But not just any something. The sugary cereals many of us eat for breakfast are worse than nothing. As I'll explain in detail in Key 5: Balanced Eating, eating big loads of sugars or starches throws your system out of whack, makes you sleepy, and leads to numerous diseases. Make sure you get some protein at breakfast; try combining that with a little fat (which keeps you full for longer) and fruits or vegetables for vitamins and fiber. Here are some good breakfast choices:

- Eggs of any kind
- Yogurt, fruit, and nuts
- Peanut butter and whole-grain toast
- Lean meat (not fatty bacon or sausage)
- Whole-grain pancakes, waffles, or muffins
- Whole-grain cereal with fruit
- Whole-grain toast with cheese

Don't skip lunch or dinner, either. Most people's bodies work best getting regular amounts of food throughout the day. But in this culture we tend to eat dinners that are way too large. Generally, we don't burn many calories after dinner, so a big dinner does little except convert into fat. Try changing the equation—eat a substantial breakfast and make dinner the lightest of the three meals—and see if that changes some other numbers, like your weight and waist measurement.

3. Drink Water

Without water you wouldn't have any energy, because water is responsible for getting nutrients from your food to your muscles and brain—via blood, which is mostly water. So are you, for that matter! We are all about two-thirds water, and we use water to do everything: to get nutrients to our cells, to cool ourselves off, to flush waste, and to circulate immune cells through the body. Without enough water, all these systems start to suffer, including metabolism. As you begin to dehydrate, you get sluggish, because the water isn't there to transfer fuel to your muscles and brain. If you want to keep your metabolism at a high level, it's essential to get enough water each day. In one German study, people's metabolisms immediately rose by 30 percent after drinking two glasses of water and stayed that way for an hour. That's a lot of extra calories burned! Read my chapter on water (Key 6) for more information. And follow this easy rule: "If you think of it, drink of it."

4. Sleep Well

Some people believe that burning the candle at both ends, staying up till all hours of the night and dragging themselves out of bed at 6 a.m. will help keep them thin, because they burn more calories during the extra wake time. Nothing is further from the truth! Sleep isn't simply "down time." Your conscience may be down, but lots of other parts of your body are hard at work, doing vital maintenance. Your brain discharges the day's stress, your body repairs injuries, and your blood restocks your muscles with fuel for the coming day. Skip this vital stage, and you drag through the day with less energy, lowered metabolism, and poor performance on everything from tests to reaction time to acting like a civilized human being. After eighteen hours of being awake, people's coordination, reaction time, judgment, and accident rates are as bad as drunk drivers.

People tend to eat more when sleep-deprived because they

feel colder and less energetic and mistake these feelings for hunger. Get a decent night's rest and you'll burn *more* calories overall—and feel a lot better about life. Tips for getting some shut-eye:

- Reduce stress. This may be the number one cause of sleeplessness.
- Exercise during the day (but not too close to bedtime).
- Have a quiet household with calming light in the evening.
- Don't drink caffeine at night.

5. Fidget

Yes, fidget. Cutting-edge research at the Mayo Clinic has found that one of the major differences between overweight people and slender people may be how much they fidget. In other words, it isn't just the planned exercise, such as walks or golf, that makes the weight difference, but the hundreds of tiny movements we make—or don't make—during the day. The Mayo Clinic researchers equipped people with special clothing containing sensors that measured every calorie they burned by moving. They found that all those little motions—getting up to look out the window, scratching your head, even shifting to the other side of the couch while watching TV—make a much bigger difference than anyone thought. The skinny people tended to "fidget away" 350 calories a day more than the overweight people. That adds up to thirty-five pounds a year!

However, you'll notice that I have not written a book called *The Fidget Diet: Your Key to Losing 35 Pounds a Year.* That's because you can't really change your built-in tendency to fidget or not to fidget. Some people are just better at being still—truly still—than others. And those people burn fewer calories because of it. People who have difficulty being still may make others nervous, but they will burn more calories than sedentary people.

Even if you can't change your unconscious tendencies, you can change the environment that allows you to avoid using your body. This is one of the easiest and most long-lasting secrets to weight loss: Don't let yourself live in ways that allow you to be still! Rebel against convenience! To be honest, I think Satan has put one over on us. He has made everything so easy and comfortable and convenient that it is killing us. We think we are saving time and effort, but we are really losing strength and energy. Doing work and staying active is not bad. Don't try to avoid it. We want drive-thru service for as many things in life as possible, but the trouble is, *there is no drive-thru good health!* Starting today, take steps to make your life a little less convenient and a little more "fidgety" or active.

> *Don't let yourself live in ways that allow you to be still! Rebel against convenience!*

Here are just a few ideas for how to do that:

- Take the stairs. Every time you skip the elevator and walk up a flight, you burn calories, tone some of the muscles you care most about toning, and wake yourself up, too.
- Don't waste time looking for the closest parking space. Park so you have to walk a little. Do it on purpose!
- Walk as much as possible. Think of ways you can get in a little extra walking.
- Don't procrastinate. When you think of a job that needs doing, get up and do it.

- Choose activities that force you to move. Try gardening, sweeping the driveway, dance classes, or mall walking.
- When you do watch TV, get up and stretch periodically. Do the same thing at work.
- Try putting your TV in front of a treadmill and slowly walk while you watch. Go slow enough that you aren't distracted. You'll be surprised how quickly it feels natural.
- I keep two five-pound exercise balls lying on the couch in my office. Several times a day, when I notice them, I stop and do a short routine to exercise my upper body. It only takes a minute or two and it loosens up tight muscles. Try it!

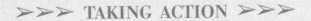

>>> TAKING ACTION >>>

"Be doers of the Word, and not hearers only."
(James 1:22)

Choose at least one action you can take to boost your metabolism. Write it down, *commit to it*, and begin today.

Action: _____

➤ KEY 4 ➤

Exercise

Whenever the word "exercise" is mentioned, everybody groans. I'll tell you a secret: I groan too! So let's not make the mistake some books and exercise programs make and pretend that exercise is always fun or convenient, and that we are all going to have a great time doing it and won't be able to stop once we get started. That certainly hasn't been my experience. I don't enjoy exercising! My husband does, but I just don't. I find walking on a treadmill to be one of the dullest tasks in life, and I'm not willing to take the time to go to a gym. (We should stop saying "I don't have the time . . ." because the truth is we can always make the time for the things most important to us. If you have the time for two or three hours of television in the evening, then you have the time to exercise, visit a friend, or do something else. When we say "I don't have the time to do that," what we really mean is, "That thing falls too far down on my priority list." And I'll be straight: visiting a gym falls *very* far down on my priority list.)

If you enjoy going out to a gym or having one in your home, by all means go for it, but fortunately gyms don't have a monopoly on exercise. There are thousands of ways to get good exercise, and most don't cost a lot of money, require special equipment, or sidetrack your day. I know that if I am going to get my exercise in, it has to be something I look forward to doing, and it has to be easy to slip into my day. I love walking two or three miles in good weather. Not only does that give me the cardiovascular workout essential for long life, it also is a great time to pray, helps me feel more energetic later, and does wonders for my stress level. I have a routine of floor exercises that I do every other day, and in general I try to make sure I move a lot. I wouldn't call myself "fidgety," but I realize the importance of being mobile. I also enjoy playing golf with my husband. It allows us a few peaceful hours together, away from the world. I get in some walking and use muscles I forgot I had.

In addition to "traditional" exercise, make an effort to keep your body active in as many small ways as possible. As I discussed in the previous chapter, these tiny things add up to big calories! Walk to a friend's house instead of driving. Use a push-mower instead of a riding mower. If you work at a computer all day, get up and take regular breaks. In addition to the hand-held exercise balls on my couch, I also have one of those huge exercise balls, and every so often I get up from my desk and bounce on the ball for five minutes. It gets the blood flowing, loosens up my spine, and gives me a break from work, which is so important.

These little breaks and forced "inconveniences" are necessary because today we use our bodies so little. We have an abundance of appliances that require us only to push a button in order to operate them. Very few of us have jobs that involve exercise, and most of our leisure activities are spent with our feet up, too. This is a new development, and a deadly one. Human beings were made to exercise. Our body is fit together with joints because God expected we would move a lot.

Admittedly, we don't hear much in the Bible about Noah's workout routine or Moses' Pilates session. Does that mean the people back then didn't get much exercise? Quite the opposite! Everything they did in life involved exercise. Before vehicles, electricity, and machines, everything in the world ran by human power or animal power. If you wanted to get somewhere, you walked. If you needed to bring something with you, you carried it. You did laundry by hand, chopped your own firewood, and milled your own grain. This physically active lifestyle may have been one of the reasons for the incredible longevity of these biblical characters.

The best walker of all may be Jesus. He routinely walked from His home in Galilee to Jerusalem—a distance of about 120 miles! Over the course of His ministry, He must have walked thousands of miles. In Jesus' day people thought little of walking ten miles. And because they did it all their lives, they had the well-developed bodies to accomplish such long walks with ease. When I was in Moscow recently, I noticed most people were slender. When I asked why, I was informed that most of them had no automobiles and walked everywhere they went.

Even as recently as 1920, people in American towns and cities walked on average nearly two miles to and from work or school, in addition to whatever exercise they got while working. That walk alone burned about 200 calories per day, which is worth twenty pounds a year in lost weight. When we traded in our daily walk for the convenience of a car, we didn't realize we were gaining twenty pounds in the bargain!

But weight loss is just the tip of the iceberg. Yes, regular exercise will help you lose weight and look your best, but there are so many health benefits from regular exercise that go beyond the value of looks. Getting in shape for show is kind of like buying a new refrigerator because you like the color. That's a fine reason, but you may come to love the great new features, super-efficiency, and extra-long-warranty even more. And you get all that through exercise. Other than not smoking, nothing can improve your health more. It truly is a magic bullet! Just a few of the conditions you can help prevent through exercise are heart disease, stroke, diabetes, cancer, Alzheimer's, arthritis, asthma, depression, and gastrointestinal ills. You'll get fewer colds, feel less stress, and you'll look great, too. Less fat, more muscle, better tone, straighter posture.

Let's take a few minutes to explore what happens when your sneaker hits the pavement and your heart starts pounding.

Keeping the Fires Burning

Ever wonder how your body stays at 98.6 degrees Fahrenheit all the time? That's a lot warmer than the air usually is. Your body pulls this off by keeping its internal fires burning. There's no flame, but otherwise all the hallmarks of a campfire are there. You need fuel, which you get from food, and oxygen, which you draw in through your lungs; and you produce heat and energy. But unlike a campfire, where all the energy is generated as heat and light, in your body a little energy is used for heat, while the rest goes to power all your systems: muscles, senses, brain, heart, and so on.

The fuel that powers your body is sugar. A particular kind of sugar called glucose is what your muscles and your brain use to keep going. Every muscle cell in your body does the same thing: it takes a molecule of glucose, burns it in a quick explosion, and uses the force of that explosion to contract. Millions of these muscle cells working together by burning glucose and contracting allow you to raise your arm, run, or even wink.

Your muscles store glucose directly in the muscle fiber, so it's there on demand. If you trip and fall, you need to get your hands in front of your face instantly, so your arms immediately burn their glucose and swing into action. But muscles can't store much glucose; only enough for a few quick actions. After that, they need to reload. The signal goes out to your body for more fuel.

That fuel is stored throughout your body in the form of fat. A fat molecule contains much more energy than a glucose molecule, so it's a better way to store extra food energy. As soon as your muscles use up their glucose supply and call for more, your body starts breaking down fat into glucose and sends it through the bloodstream to the muscles that need it.

The process of breaking down fat requires oxygen. That makes it easy to tell when your muscles have used up their own glucose and are getting more fuel from fat: you start to breathe harder, because you need the oxygen. This usually happens after one to two minutes of any aerobic activity. (*Aerobic* means oxygen-using. Aerobic exercises are those that involve sustained activity, such as walking, jogging, or bike riding, but not quick bursts like hitting a baseball or lifting a weight.) Any time you feel yourself breathing hard during a workout, pat yourself on the back; it means you are literally burning fat.

If you exercise so hard, however, that you are gasping for breath, then your body can't keep up with your oxygen demands. Without the oxygen, it doesn't do a very good job of completely burning the fat and leaves behind a nasty waste product called lactic acid. Just like the painful feeling of acid on a cut, lactic acid in your muscle doesn't feel very good—it's that sore feeling you get a day after overworking a muscle. Better to slow down so that you're breathing hard but not gasping.

A good way to picture all this is to think of your charcoal grill. The lighter fluid is like the glucose that burns right away but doesn't last long; after a minute or so, it's used up and you need the charcoal briquettes (fat) that can burn for hours. And if you cut off your grill's air intake, the charcoal smolders and leaves behind unburned residue (lactic acid).

The Heart of the Matter

As you can see, energy for exercise depends on getting enough oxygen and fuel to your muscles, and both those things are accomplished through the bloodstream. Blood is your transportation network, and your heart drives that network. As your demand for fuel and air increases, your heart pumps faster and faster, speeding the blood along on its important delivery route. Your blood vessels that feed your exercising muscles dilate too, so they can carry more blood where it's needed.

Exercise once, and your whole system goes back to normal when you stop. Exercise regularly for a couple of weeks, and things begin to change. Remember, God gave you a body of incredible adaptability. It molds itself to your lifestyle, to make it easier for you to accomplish whatever you're working on. As muscles get used, they get bigger and stronger—including the heart. A stronger heart pumps more blood with less stress. Blood vessels also get stronger through exercise. The walls of your arteries have a layer of smooth muscle in them which dilates and contracts the arteries as needed. That's how your body adjusts the amount of blood that goes to any particular area. If you run, the arteries that go to your legs dilate so more blood flows to your leg muscle. You don't control these arterial muscles any more than you do your heart, but they just as surely get a workout when you exercise. The regular dilation keeps artery walls supple and flexible, so they can dilate wide when needed and are less likely to develop dangerous cholesterol buildups and blockages. Blood vessels to muscles that aren't being used contract, in order to avoid wasting blood where it's not needed.

Now you understand why regular exercise as simple as walking a couple of miles most days can cut your risk of heart attack and stroke *in half!* A heart attack happens when cholesterol builds up on artery walls and eventually blocks the flow of blood to the heart. A stroke is the same occurrence in a blood vessel going to the brain. The very best way to prevent these and other forms of cardiovascular disease is steady, moderate exercise, which keeps your blood vessels wide and clear and your heart big and strong.

The Diabetes Epidemic

Now that you know how the cardiovascular system works, you'll see why diabetes is even easier to prevent than heart disease through diet and exercise. Good thing, because diabetes is out of control in America. An astounding twenty million Americans have diabetes, and more than forty million are prediabetic, meaning they have all the conditions in place to develop the disease unless they quickly make lifestyle changes.

Diabetes is a sugar disease. It is caused by high levels of glucose in the blood, the result of a diet high in fat, sugars, and starches, along with a sedentary lifestyle. You'd think raised glucose in the blood is a good thing—more energy!—but elevated glucose levels over a long time cause lots of problems. You know how sugary sauces get syrupy and sticky? Well, when your blood has too much glucose, it gets sticky, too. Then it's more likely to damage artery walls and form the clots that cause cardiovascular disease. Most diabetics will eventually die from heart disease or stroke. They are also more likely to suffer from Alzheimer's disease (high glucose levels in the brain cause memory loss and dementia), kidney failure, and blindness.

It seems like the muscles would absorb any extra glucose in the blood—and they try, but they can only take so much. Insulin is the factor. It's a hormone, made by the pancreas that acts like a key, getting muscle cells to open up and absorb some glucose. The more glucose in the blood, the more insulin the pancreas makes, and all that insulin zips around, desperately trying to get your muscles to take more and more glucose. But eventually they get stuffed and resist. This is called "insulin resistance."

When the muscles resist, all that glucose is left in the blood. Your body then converts the glucose to fat and desperately crams it into fat cells, but they start to resist after a while too. Assuming more and more sugars and starches are coming in by way of the mouth, glucose levels in the blood keep rising, and the pancreas pumps out insulin faster and faster. But there's nowhere for the glucose to go, and eventually the overworked pancreas breaks down. Then there is NO way of getting any glucose into muscle cells, and you have a full-blown case of diabetes.

Preventing diabetes depends on controlling both sides of the equation: the rate that sugars and starches come into the body and the rate that glucose is burned up by the muscles. The less you eat, the less glucose goes into the blood; the more you exercise, the more your muscles burn off their glucose supply and need a refill. Regular exercise "trains" your muscles to cooperate with insulin to open up to more glucose; it reduces insulin resistance.

A steady exercise program reduces your chance of contracting diabetes by nearly two-thirds. Combined with a healthy diet, low in sugars, starches, and saturated fat, it makes your risk of diabetes negligible. If you already have diabetes, no amount of exercise will restart your pancreas, but it will still help control your glucose levels and allow you to take as little insulin as possible.

Cancer and the Immune System

The connection between exercise and cancer protection is not as direct as that between exercise and reduced cardiovascular disease. Exercise has little impact on some cancers, yet it reduces your risk of breast cancer by thirty-seven percent and has similar protection against prostate and colon cancer. It does this by stimulating your immune system. Your immune defense, centered in the lymphatic system, circulates white blood cells through the body, where they find and eliminate any cellular threats, such as bacteria, viruses, and cancer cells. Unlike blood, which is pumped through the body by the heart, lymph depends on muscle contractions to squeeze it through the body. Moderate exercise more than doubles the rate at which your lymph circulates! The faster those white blood cells circulate, the more cancer cells and viruses they can pick off.

Stress

Stress is simply anything that requires us to react. Our body responds by sending hormones like adrenaline and cortisol through the blood to improve our performance level. Our breathing and heart rate increase, which means more fuel for the muscles and brain. We think faster, react quicker, and have extra strength. This is great, if the stressor is infrequent and if we have some outlet for reacting: running, delivering a sensational performance on stage, or in some other way being *active*. However, all too often in the modern world we have no physical outlet for the stress. Our boss yells at us in a meeting, we have a fight with our spouse, and we can do nothing but sit there, hormones surging, arteries taking a beating, blood super-charged with oxygen, all bottled up inside. For reasons I'll explain in depth in Key 9: De-Stress, constant stress is a quick ticket to the grave. Driving your car down the highway at 65 mph is fine, but run your car in park in your driveway, press the gas pedal to the floor, and it won't be long before your engine overheats.

When we experience stress (and let's face it, most of us deal with it every day) the best thing we can do is what our bodies scream at us to do anyway: *Move!* Exercise is the best stress-reducer known to man. It burns up that extra adrenaline and gets our bodies back to a relaxed state, which means you can spend your night sleeping instead of seething.

Depression

We've all heard of the "runner's high." It turns out it's true, and so is "golfer's high" and "walker's high." Exercise has an aston-ishing effect on depression. Studies show that a half-hour a day of moderate exercise is as effective in relieving mild depression as antidepressants! This modest exercise even helps some people who don't respond to antidepressants.

How does exercise do this? One way is by triggering the release of endorphins, chemicals in the brain that are respon-sible for good moods. Perhaps the brain does this to compen-sate for the sore muscles exercise can cause. No one knows for sure. But I believe the better self-esteem we feel when we exer-cise is as responsible as the endorphins. Whatever the reason, it's another one of God's ways that works—and that's all we really need to know.

Osteoporosis

Osteoporosis means *porous brittle bones,* and it happens to all of us as we age, women in particular. Starting in their thirties, women lose bone mass every year. *Unless.* And that "unless" is exercise. Regular exercise can preserve the same bone strength you had in your thirties throughout your life.

Although we're not aware of it, our bones constantly change. Bones use calcium as their building blocks, and the more the muscles attached to the bone get used, the stronger your body makes those bones by reinforcing them with extra calcium. But if your bones aren't frequently "tested" by the force of muscle upon them, your body assumes they aren't that vital for your lifestyle, and it doesn't reinforce them. Then the calcium in them slowly erodes. Bones of sedentary older women are honeycombed, with more hole than bone. It doesn't take much of a fall to make them crumble, and then healing is slow or non-existent.

The good news is that the power to avoid osteoporosis is completely in your grasp. As you age, take a multivitamin with calcium to make sure your body has the raw materials it needs to build fresh bone. And make sure you exercise *all* your muscles frequently. Walking or running is great for your lower half, but it won't help your upper body much. Strength training, using simple hand weights or resistance bands, is a great way to get the upper body involved. Swimming works well, too.

Five Ways to Get Started

The toughest thing about a new exercise program is that first mile. If it has been years since you exercised, every step can feel like torture. Everybody seems to be

> *The toughest thing about a new exercise program is that first mile.*

in better shape than you. Completing a three-mile walk seems utterly impossible; you feel lucky to drag yourself a half-mile.

The answer, of course, is that a half-mile is just fine. In the long run, what makes the big difference is not starting off with a five-mile run but continual progress in the right direction, along with *meeting your goals.* Quitting before you've accomplished your goal can become a slippery slope. That's why it's much better to begin with attainable goals and reach them than to set for yourself unrealistic tasks and give up part way. Following are five extremely simple ways many people have found to begin exercise programs that stick.

1. A Daily Walk

Experts used to think that you had to work up a good sweat to get the true health benefits of exercise. Walking was a fine way to take a break, but true exercise meant running, aerobic workouts, or other intense sports. Wrong! Researchers now know that most of the health benefits of exercise come from something as simple as thirty minutes of walking every day. More intense exercise will burn more calories, and you'll lose more weight, but you won't increase your longevity or disease protection much. In fact, extended exercise can actually depress your immune system.

Thirty minutes of walking means about two miles at a

standard walking pace. You don't have to start out doing this much. If fifteen minutes leaves you gasping, that's all you need for starters. Work your way up to thirty, and do it at least five days a week. Eventually, two miles may seem too easy to you; try pushing it up to three, or do two very fast miles. Keep yourself mildly challenged. Feel free to walk longer than thirty minutes, though most people find that a half hour is about all they can devote to exercise on a busy day. If you like to use a book for guidance, try Dr. Don Colbert's *Walking in Divine Health.*

Worried that you'll find excuses to avoid that walk? Then get a dog. He'll let you know if you haven't walked that day, I assure you!

2. Indoor Exercise

I'm an outdoor walker. I love the chance to experience the day and the changing seasons from a path or a fairway. Others find it too hard to maintain an outdoor exercise program year-round. In Florida, summer walks are unbearable. In Michigan, winter walks require bundling up, hunkering down, and dodging ice patches. No matter where they live, many people are more comfortable exercising in the privacy of their own homes using workout videos. Many classic aerobics videos are available, and if these seem too strenuous for you, there are videos that combine walking-in-place with simple strength-training moves to give a gentle, all-body workout. Of particular interest are Leslie Sansone's *Walk the Walk* videos, which combine walking with a soundtrack of Christian spirituals to provide a workout that firms the body *and* uplifts the soul. If you like classes, there are aerobics classes offered in every city these days. Whatever your tastes, there is a program out there for you. Don't let the outdoors stop you from exercising!

3. Strength Training

As I explained in this chapter, aerobic exercises such as walking or bike riding burn calories, improve cardiovascular function, and chase the blues away, but they don't provide much help against osteoporosis in the upper body. That requires quick, intense muscle work such as weight-lifting, strength training, and sit-ups. The great thing about strength-training programs is that they can be done at home in just a few minutes a day and require no special equipment. Many books and videos are available. Find one that fits your needs, and keep those bones and muscles strong.

4. Running or Biking

Some people get bored walking. If you know you need exercise, but know that you won't stay enthusiastic about it unless the world starts flying by, then I suggest you try running or biking. A lot of people love biking, and it's much easier on your joints than running is. Cities and towns are much better than they used to be about maintaining bike lanes and paths. You may find that quite a few errands can be accomplished on a bike that you used to do by car, meaning your exercise isn't taking up any extra time.

5. Swimming

If you are part of the minority of people whose physical problems prevent you from even trying a daily walk, you can still exercise! Many city pools offer water aerobics classes, and simply swimming laps is one of the healthiest activities you can do. Swimming takes all the weight off the body. It works many different muscles and provides a gentle cardiovascular workout without any joint or bone stress. And indoor pools make it a convenient option year-round.

➤➤➤ TAKING ACTION ➤➤➤

"Be doers of the Word, and not hearers only."
(James 1:22)

Choose at least one action you can take to get more exercise in your life. Write it down, *commit to it,* and begin today.

Action: _____

➤ KEY 5 ➤

Balanced Eating

After God created Adam and Eve, He gave them some very simple dining instructions. "You may freely eat of every tree in the garden," He said in Genesis 2:16.

Did He say, "You may freely eat of every Krispy Kreme on the street"? No. Did He say, "You may freely eat of every chip in the bag"? No. He did not tell them to freely eat fast food, frozen pizza, or even low-fat cookies.

God told Adam and Eve to eat from the garden, and we'd do well to stick to His advice. We've been inundated with an overwhelming amount of bad diet information from past decades, which has clouded the very simple truths of healthy eating: eat the foods that come from God, in a state as close as possible to how God made them, and you can't go wrong. Only when we get corrupted by the foods made by men in laboratories and factories do we get in trouble. Our bodies were not designed to get their nutrition in these forms. As I'll explain in this chapter, our bodies still don't know what to do with these processed foods.

Once when I was teaching on the subject of food, I asked the congregation to repeat after me, "I am free to eat!" You should have seen the fear cross many faces. So often people struggle with weight, live in bondage to food and food cravings, and believe for years that they are most certainly *not* free to eat! Quite the opposite; for them, meals come with all the rules and trepidation of military school. But as you know, when anyone's spirit is oppressed by too many rules and directives, it longs for freedom. It rebels!

That is one reason why so many diets fail. They are all about restrictions. And the human spirit is designed for freedom. Which is why "I am free to eat!" is such a powerful message, and such an unsettling one for some people. They want to believe it, but they have had the opposite message driven into them for too long.

YOU ARE FREE TO EAT! Believe it. In this chapter you will learn why. You will unlearn all the unhelpful things you have been taught about diet, and you are going to begin a joyful, easy, guilt-free routine of freely eating the good foods God has put on earth for you. No calorie-counting, no tracked servings of this or that food group, no worried glances at the nutritional information on the back of packages.

The Low-Fat Catastrophe

Here we are, scarred veterans of the Low-Fat Wars of the eighties and nineties. You remember this era. I know I do! All the smart nutritionists told us that fat was the enemy. They told us that if we could just cut the fat in our diet we would lose weight. Soon hordes of low-fat products appeared on store shelves to help us: low-fat cookies, low-fat ice cream, low-fat cheese and chips and frozen dinners.

And we obeyed. We cut the butter, the oil, the meat and the

mayo. We ate every low-fat product known to man. And you know what happened?

We got fatter. The percentage of obese Americans doubled in those two decades from fifteen percent to thirty percent. The percentage of overweight children *tripled*. Women now eat 335 more calories per day than they did thirty years ago.

How can this be? How can we have cut fat and gained weight? (And blown our rates of heart disease and diabetes through the roof?)

The answer is that when nutritionists told us to cut fat, they simply did not know what they were talking about. The whole notion that fat made us fat came from the knowledge that, ounce for ounce, fat has more than twice as many calories as protein or carbohydrates. So replace the fat with an equal weight of something else, and we eat fewer calories, right?

Well, technically, yes. When low-fat diet advocates studied people in the lab, prepared their meals and measured every calorie they consumed, replacing grams of fat with grams of carbs worked just fine. The people lost weight. However, they were also starving, distracted and grumpy. That wasn't part of the study. The message went out far and wide: low-fat, high-carb is your ticket to health and weight-loss! Fat is a dirty word!

And we listened. The percentage of calories we get from fat has dropped from thirty-seven percent to thirty-two, while the percentage of calories we get from carbohydrates has risen from forty-five percent to fifty-two.

Unfortunately, things got more complicated when real people started trying this diet. Sure, a gram of carbohydrates has fewer calories than a gram of fat, but it turns out that doesn't help much, because the gram of fat is much better at making you feel full. The carbohydrate just makes you want more.

Remember when we compared your food to fuel for a grill? Sugar (which the body converts to glucose) is the lighter fluid that burns fast and hot, while fat is the briquette that burns long and slow. Carbohydrates are types of sugar molecules. When these sugar molecules are by themselves they taste sweet, like sugar or honey, but sometimes they stick together in long chains. Starches, such as flour, corn, or potatoes, are simply long chains of sugar molecules. They don't taste sweet on our tongue because they are too big to fit onto our sugar taste buds, but the body breaks them down into sugar molecules almost instantly. Machines can do it, too: corn is a starch that doesn't taste very sweet, and corn syrup is the exact same stuff broken down into little bits.

No matter what type of carbohydrate you put in your body— french fries or bread or cotton candy—it gets dumped into the blood as glucose for energy. If your muscles happen to be in use that moment, they'll have plenty of energy. (This is why athletes like to eat carbohydrates before competing.) If not, well, your body can always convert all that glucose to fat and store it.

Either way, eating a big load of pasta or cake causes your blood sugar level to soar. And your body responds by making tons of insulin, that hormone that makes the muscle cells or fat cells open up to receive the sugar. But having so much insulin in your blood means that your body is a little too effective at storing the sugar somewhere and you swing from very high blood sugar levels to very low ones.

Low blood sugar is also known as hypoglycemia. And you know the feeling of low blood sugar: hunger. You feel hungry, your concentration drops, you get grumpy and weak and low in energy. All you can think about is food.

So you eat. And if what you eat is mostly carbohydrates, then your blood sugar soars again, you make a lot more insulin, and the whole process repeats itself. (Until, of course, your pancreas gets so exhausted from making all the insulin that it breaks down and you get diabetes.)

Many of us spent a good deal of the low-fat eighties and nineties on this blood-sugar roller coaster, soaring on surges of carbohydrates and crashing in hunger two hours later. Snacking on a baked potato—with sugary, low-fat dressing—then looking up from our desks an hour later thinking, "I can't believe I'm hungry again." So we wound up snacking constantly, consuming more calories per day than ever before, even though less of the calories were in the form of fat. And we gained weight.

Letting the Body Do Its Job

Why aren't our bodies better at regulating what they need? Did God design us all to be fat? Of course He didn't. Our bodies are *excellent* at regulating their needs, but this world of donuts and cotton candy is something they've never had to deal with before. Until a few hundred years ago, when crops such as sugarcane and potatoes became readily available, there were very few convenient forms of carbohydrates for us to eat. There was fruit, and every once in a while somebody would be brave enough to raid a honeycomb, but that was pretty much it in terms of sweets. Other carbohydrates came from vegetables and grains, such as wheat and oats. People made bread, porridge, and other foods from those grains, but in a very different form from how we see bread today.

People ate *whole grains,* the natural seed part of the plant. Think of oats or barley and you've got a good sense of whole grains: chewy, tough outsides, soft insides. Then somebody came along and invented machines that stripped off the chewy outer part of the grain, leaving the soft inner part. That's what white flour is: the delicate inside part without the outer shell. Whole wheat, on the other hand, is the whole grain.

There's no denying that we love the delicate, creamy taste of bread, pastry, and other foods made with white flour. And there's no point in even discussing our built-in taste for refined sugar! But these are the types of foods that cause the massive insulin response in our bodies I described above, which leads to overeating, obesity, cardiovascular disease, and diabetes.

Why don't whole grains cause this same reaction? Because of that fibrous outer shell. It takes your digestive system time to strip that shell off to get to the goodies inside, which means the rate at which the carbohydrates are delivered into the blood is slowed down considerably. And that means blood sugar levels stay nice and steady. You stay full longer, as your body slowly works through those tough whole grains. It's like giving your dog a chew toy. You don't give him a paper chew toy, because he'll tear it up in seconds and be begging for another. You give him one of those ultra-tough rawhide bones that keep him busy for hours. Give your body the tough foods it was designed to digest and it will stay busy for hours, too, leaving you free to have a life.

Vegetables and even fruit also keep their carbohydrates wrapped up in fibrous packages, requiring our bodies to work longer to get it. These packages also contain the vitamins and minerals we need, which are in whole grains as well but sorely lacking from refined flour and sugar.

Nutrients Stripped Away to Make White Flour		
fiber	niacin	thiamin
iron	phosphorus	vitamin B_6
magnesium	potassium	vitamin E
manganese	riboflavin	zinc

And what about the fiber in whole grains? It's indigestible, so it passes right through the body unabsorbed. This means it's calorie-free, so if you take two foods of the same size, the one with more fiber (and water) will be lower in calories. That's why a piece of fruit, which is high in water and fiber, has far fewer calories than a candy bar.

In some cases fiber can be counted as *negative* calories, because it absorbs fat in your food and carries it out of the body. This reduces your calorie intake, as well as your cholesterol level and your risk of cardiovascular disease. Fiber also acts like a Roto-Rooter in your intestines, preventing blockages.

Fiber is miraculous! It's also very mundane. It's present in most plant foods in their natural state. Only when we use technology to do things to food that God never intended, are we able to create foods that *hurt* the body. Higher fiber content slows down the rate at which a food's carbohydrates are absorbed into our blood stream, as does the softness of the food. (Our bodies take a lot longer to soften up a piece of raw broccoli and get the carbohydrates out of it than they do broccoli that's been cooked to mush.) The size of the food matters, too. Even whole wheat bread can be absorbed quickly if mills have pulverized the whole grains into fine powder. That's why you want to look for multigrain bread with lots of chewy, crunchy bits in it.

The common theme in this discussion is that you should get in the way of nature as little as possible. God gave you a vast garden of healthy foods to eat, and a body fully capable of dealing with those foods. You have teeth for ripping and grinding your food, a stomach that soaks food in water and acid and throws it around like Hulk Hogan until it falls to pieces, and an intestine that takes those small pieces and extracts every last bit of goodness from them. Your body *wants* to do this; people have done this for thousands of years. When you let machines do the ripping and grinding and softening and pre-digesting, your body doesn't get to do the job it was made for, and disease is the result.

Does Fat Make Me Fat?

When the Low-Fat Police of the eighties and nineties told us to cut fat from our diets, it was because fat is such a concentrated source of calories. Fat has nine calories per gram, while protein and carbohydrates have just four. Not understanding the body's response to carbohydrates, which I've described above, they believed we'd consume fewer calories and lose weight. It seemed logical: if our problem is too much fat *on* our bodies, we should take less fat *into* those bodies!

But it turns out fat tends to make us full. It's the charcoal briquettes that burn long and slow. Yes, it's a more concentrated form of calories, but we tend to eat it in small amounts. (How much olive oil can you chug?) Fat molecules are more complex than carbohydrates, so our bodies take a lot longer to dismantle them and get the calories. Just like high-fiber whole grains, a little keeps our body working longer.

Perhaps most important of all, fat has compounds in it called leptins, the signal the brain looks for to know you are full. When the intestine detects leptins, it sends a message to the brain saying "All set! We got what we needed. Stop eating." It takes about twenty minutes from the time we eat for food to clear our stomach and reach our small intestine, where the leptin signal is sent, and suddenly our brain tells us we're full. That's why the classic advice is to wait twenty minutes after eating to decide if you're full or not. But you need to eat some fat with your food to make this happen. (And you get into trouble if you eat so quickly that by the time the first food hits your small intestine and triggers the leptins, you already have stuffed a huge amount of food into the pipeline.)

This new understanding of the role of fat and carbohydrates in regulating appetite was the reasoning behind the wave of low-carb diets. Keep your insulin response down by avoiding carbs, eat enough protein and fat to keep yourself full and on an even keel, and you'll eat fewer calories overall and lose weight.

You know what? They may be right! You can lose weight on low-carb diets—*if* you can stay on them! Not an easy task in a world that constantly offers carbohydrates in convenient forms. Check out the offerings next time you're in a convenience store: chips, pretzels, candy, cookies, muffins, ice cream, popsicles, slurpies, sodas, juices. All carbohydrates. How *convenient*. Unless you consider disease inconvenient.

Some low-carb diets go too far, telling you to cut out healthy sources of carbohydrates such as fruit and whole grains. Some also make the mistake of implying that all fats are alike. As I'll explain in the next section, they most definitely are not.

Does Fat Make Me Sick?

Researchers had a second reason for telling us to eat less fat, and this time they were on to something. They thought it would make us healthier. Clogged arteries, they knew, come from fatty compounds like cholesterol that stick together in our bloodstream and then stick to the walls of the arteries, forming a blockage. If a blockage cuts off blood to our heart, we suffer a heart attack. If it cuts off blood to our brain, we suffer a stroke.

Our bodies manufacture cholesterol from the fat in the food we eat. This seems like a pretty good reason to cut out fat! But when people actually went on low-fat diets, their rate of heart disease often went up! Why? As it turns out, there are two kinds of cholesterol. One is bad (LDL cholesterol) and forms the plaque that clogs our arteries; the other is good (HDL cholesterol) and helps sweep those arteries clear.

We now know that different types of fat have different effects on our cholesterol levels. Some raise the bad cholesterol level and lower the good, some do the opposite, and some lower all cholesterol levels. The people on low-fat diets were cutting down on the dangerous type of fat, but cutting the protective form of fat, too.

There's an easy way to determine whether a fat is likely to contribute to clogged arteries. Is it solid or liquid at body temperature? In a 98-degree room, does it look like oil or bacon fat? Fats that are solid or semi-solid will be that way in your body, too, meaning they are much more likely to stick and form plaque. These fats, known as saturated fats, are all from mammals: beef, pork, lamb, and dairy. They are the ones that raise bad cholesterol and contribute to heart disease.

Fats that are liquid at body temperature, however, are some of the healthiest foods you can eat. These unsaturated fats lower the bad cholesterol that causes plaque, raise the good cholesterol that prevents it, and keep the entire body running smoothly. Olive oil leads the pack, along with fish oil and canola oil. Other plant oils are less healthy but much better than saturated fat.

Switching from saturated fat to unsaturated fat can make a huge difference in your health. Even a small start produces big results. Switching just 100 calories per day in your diet—less than a tablespoon—from a solid fat to olive oil can cut your risk of heart attack *in half*. Cut back on most red meat and whole-fat dairy, eat more fish and olive oil, and your risk goes down even further. This is the basis of the now-famous Mediterranean Diet, and it's a proven life-extender. Switching to a Mediterranean Diet and exercising regularly reduces your risk of heart disease by eighty percent! It's no coincidence that this diet is also the basic diet consumed by the people of biblical times:

lots of fruits, vegetables, whole grains, and fish, with occasional red meat and poultry and very little dairy (mostly yogurt). It's got quite a track record!

Embrace the Old Bad Guys

It's amazing how many of the foods we were told not to eat in the eighties and nineties have turned out to be good for us. Look at this list of the falsely accused, now all considered health food—when eaten in moderation.

Chocolate

Coffee

Olive oil

Canola oil

Peanut butter

Sunflower seeds

Walnuts and cashews

Avocados

Eggs

Other Benefits of Fat

The bottom line is that you don't need to worry about getting less fat in your diet. You need fat! In addition to the cardiovascular benefits, fat is essential for healthy, supple skin and a functioning brain. It pads your organs and helps keep you warm. The essential fatty acids (EFAs) found in fish, nuts, and vegetable fats keep cell walls from breaking, thin the blood, regulate blood pressure, reduce inflammation, and improve the immune system. Omega-3 fatty acids, found in oily fish such as salmon and mackerel, are especially effective at protecting against heart disease.

We haven't even mentioned the most important benefit of fat, which is that it tastes great! Without fat, in fact, food tastes pretty hollow. It still tastes sweet, salty, or spicy, but it has little depth or aroma, because fat carries flavor. You know this from how lousy most low-fat products taste. (Companies usually add a lot of extra sugar to try to make up for the lost flavor.) Food that doesn't have flavor is not satisfying, and since we ultimately eat to be satisfied, we are more likely to overeat food that is sweet or salty but unsatisfying, because we never get that contentment we are craving.

Rather than less fat, your goal should be to cut as much saturated fat as possible from your diet and replace it with unsaturated fat. Eating balanced, nutritious, well-flavored food means eating some fat. How many ways can you think of to work olive oil, nuts, fish, and avocados into your meals?

Natural Fats

My general rule of choosing foods in a form as close as possible to how God provided them is especially important with fats. All the olive oil you eat should be extra-virgin. This means the oil was pressed directly out of fresh olives, as has been done for millennia. Non-virgin oil has been extracted from inferior olives or old olive pulp using heat, solvents, other chemicals, and sometimes bleaches. It has few health benefits.

Vegetable oils extracted from grains and legumes follow a similar process to non-virgin olive oil. Unlike a ripe olive or nut, which practically oozes oil, grains lock up their oil much tighter. If you've ever tried to squeeze oil from corn or soybeans, you probably haven't had much luck. Factories heat the plants to extremely high temperatures to break down their structure and force the oil out, then add chemical solvents to dissolve the plants further. *Then* they increase the temperature to cook off the solvents. What's left looks pretty unappetizing, so they bleach and deodorize it to make it something consumers will buy. At this point, not only have all nutrients been destroyed, but dangerous oxidation has happened. This is why I recommend sticking to extra-virgin olive oil or other oils marked "cold-pressed" for your oil needs.

Even the animals we depend on for meat have become less healthy, thanks to industrialization. When people in biblical times ate cattle or lamb, they were eating animals that roamed freely on pastureland, eating fresh grass and other green plants. Now these animals (as well as poultry) are raised on factory farms, getting little or no exercise and eating mostly grain residue. These animals have much more unhealthy fat than their lean and active biblical counterparts, and fewer of the vitamins and antioxidants that come from eating fresh greens. They are also fed antibiotics to keep them from spreading diseases through the close quarters in which they are kept. Chances are red meat was much healthier for us back when the animals led natural lives. Look for meat labeled "grass-fed," "free-range," or "organic" if you want to truly emulate a biblical diet.

Protein

So far we have discussed carbohydrates and fat but haven't mentioned the most important nutrient of them all—protein. Carbs and fat provide your fuel and do the other special jobs

Trans-Fat

The most dangerous fats of all don't exist in nature anywhere. They are trans-fats, which are made by taking vegetable oils, which are unsaturated fats, and *trans*forming them into saturated fats. Why would anyone do such a thing? Because saturated fats don't go rancid as quickly, so they improve the shelf life of all processed foods that contain fat, such as margarine, chips, cookies, crackers, baked goods, and peanut butter. But when you learn the process by which trans-fats are made, you'll want to stay far away from them. The vegetable oils are superheated, then hydrogen gas is bubbled through them until they harden. Ugh! (Because of the hydrogen process, these oils are called *hydrogenated oils;* you'll see this ingredient in many foods.) Trans-fats are even more likely to cause heart disease than normal saturated fat. Now the USDA has recognized the dangers of trans-fats and required that they be listed on the nutrition information on every food package. Only buy foods that are free of trans-fat.

I've mentioned, but protein builds you. You *are* protein. Your muscles are protein, your organs, your DNA, your hormones, and part of your bones, too. Many of the specialized tasks performed by your body are handled by protein molecules. To keep yourself operating at peak efficiency, and to rebuild tissue as it breaks down, you need a steady supply of protein each day.

Nobody has found much bad to say about protein. It doesn't cause heart disease, make you fat, or even make you sleepy. I've learned that I need a high percentage of protein in my diet. I love pasta and could eat it every day, but a big plate of spaghetti always makes me sleepy afterward. If I want to get anything done with my afternoon, I've learned to steer clear of too many starches and eat a high-protein lunch. I stay alert and healthy, and I feel good. Like fat, protein takes a while for your digestive system to break down, so it's better at keeping you full than carbohydrates are.

The most obvious form of protein is animal flesh. Other than the fat, animal flesh is all protein. Eggs are another excellent source. Dairy is high in protein, but also often high in saturated fat, as is red meat. Nuts, beans, and seeds have a terrific mix of protein, fiber, vitamins, and other essential nutrients, with no saturated fat. We would do well to replace some of our red meat consumption with these plant sources of protein, along with fish, chicken, and turkey.

Nature's Pharmacy

Not only did God provide all the nutrients we need for a lifetime of health, but He provided the medicines we need, too. Every day scientists discover new healing compounds in fruits and vegetables. The first of these to be discovered are the vitamins we are all familiar with, but now scientists realize that a vast array of compounds called *antioxidants* are just as essential to our health. Different types of antioxidants are found in all fruits and vegetables, and they protect different parts of the body, but they all work by preventing damage done by *free radicals* and other toxins in the environment. These toxins attack our cells and DNA, causing everything from heart disease and cancer to eye disease, Alzheimer's, and sagging skin. But antioxidants are able to bind with the toxins, neutralize them, and remove them from the body. The more antioxidants we eat, the more protected we are against disease and the effects of aging. Every time you eat fruits and vegetables, you buy yourself more time. Eat them at every meal, and soon you will have slowed down the aging process significantly.

Our understanding of antioxidants and other micronutrients is still evolving, so your safest bet is to eat a variety of fruits and vegetables daily. Don't just take vitamin pills, even if they say they have antioxidants, because natural foods contain hundreds, maybe thousands of disease-fighting compounds we haven't yet identified, and those aren't in the pills. And these compounds may work best in the combinations God provided. Nutritional supplements are important, but work best when taken with the foods God intended us to eat.

Here is a list of various fruits and vegetables and what they are particularly good at preventing:

Broccoli, cabbage, Brussels sprouts	→ Colon cancer, heart disease
Spinach, collards, other greens	→ Colon cancer, stomach cancer, eye diseases, heart disease
Onions, garlic, leeks, shallots	→ Stomach cancer, heart disease
Carrots, sweet potatoes, squash	→ Breast, stomach, mouth, throat, and lung cancer
Tomatoes, watermelon	→ Prostate, stomach, and lung cancer

Blueberries, strawberries,   ⟶   Cardiovascular disease
apples, red grapes, red
cabbage, chocolate
(no sugar), beets, plums

In addition to what they have in them, natural foods are also important for what they *don't* have. No antibiotics, dyes, or preservatives. No artificial flavors or carcinogenic chemicals. No lab-created "fake fats" or indigestible sugar substitutes. Many of the five-syllable ingredients you see on the ingredients lists of packaged foods haven't been proven to be dangerous— but they haven't been proven safe, either.

Cholesterol in Food: False Alarm

Once scientists learned that the cholesterol in our blood was responsible for clogged arteries, the alarm was sounded to avoid foods high in cholesterol. Eggs were the worst culprit, and suddenly egg consumption plummeted as people thought of them as "a heart attack on a plate." But it turns out there was no cause for alarm. Eggs do not raise your risk of heart disease. In fact, there is almost no connection between the cholesterol you eat and the cholesterol level of your blood. Your body manufactures cholesterol from saturated fat and transfats, and those are what you want to avoid in food. Don't worry about cholesterol content in food, and don't worry about eating eggs. They are actually one of nature's most perfect foods, full of protein, healthy fat, and hard-to-get vitamins such as D and B_{12}. Just don't fry them in lots of butter and melt a hefty slice of cheese over the top!

The Goal: Balance

When I talked about investing in your health, I told you that you were going to have to invest a little time in learning about healthy foods to eat, and perhaps this chapter has tested you. I've given you a lot of information. Most people don't like blindly marching to someone else's orders; they are much more willing to do something if they understand why they are doing it. Now that you see the way different types of foods affect the body, I hope you understand why it is so important—yet so easy—to eat a healthy, balanced diet. The Bible tells us to remain balanced so that the devil cannot find an entrance into our lives (1 Peter 5:8). Excess is the devil's playground.

As in all areas of life, common sense is key. It's absurd to think that one cookie will bring your health crashing down. It's equally absurd to think that you can eat a full dessert twice every day with no consequences. Moderation is the right path in all things. If you can eat an occasional sweet, at birthday parties or dinner parties, that is a perfectly wonderful part of

Moderation is the right path in all things.

life. But a friend of mine says she absolutely cannot eat even one cookie without eating the whole box, so she knows not to have that one cookie. The Bible says if your eye offends you, then pluck it out (Matthew 18:9). What this means is that if one thing in life is threatening your downfall, you need to cut that thing out of your life.

We don't need to go to such extremes usually. A little sugar won't kill you. Neither will a little pasta, white bread, bacon, or filet mignon. Most of us are mature enough to mix the occasional indulgence into a general pattern of wholesome, balanced meals.

Look for that balance on your plate. A variety of color is one good sign; it means you're getting a nice mix of vitamins and antioxidants. Allow yourself some carbohydrates for energy—preferably whole-grain ones like brown rice, whole wheat, corn kernels, or beans—but make sure they are balanced by plenty of protein and healthy fat, such as olive oil or avocado. Even if you eat refined carbohydrates, such as sugar or white rice, eating protein and fat at the same time will mix everything in your stomach and delay the rate at which your body can absorb the carbohydrates—meaning less of a blood-sugar spike. That's why a little ice cream is a better idea than a donut by itself in the middle of the afternoon. The protein in the ice cream helps.

Above all, *don't stress over what you eat.* The purpose of all the information I've given you in this chapter is not to overwhelm you with worries about tracking the nutrition content of every morsel you put in your mouth; it's to get you to realize that eating healthy simply involves rotating a variety of good foods through your week. Most foods are good for you! Just don't fall into the American habit of relying too heavily on a few—beef, potato, sugar, and so on—that should be consumed only once or twice a week. As long as God's cornucopia crosses your plate each week, and most of it looks more or less like it did when it came from the farm, you will be just fine.

Five Ways to Put Balanced Eating into Practice

It's one thing to say "Eat more vegetables, fruit, and whole grains; eat less red meat, white flour, and dessert." It's another thing to make that happen.

1. *Make Food Sacred*

Learn to do everything you do for God's glory, including eating. Look at your dinner plate and ask if what you are about to eat is mostly what God created for you. Don't view eating as a secular event that has nothing to do with your relationship with God. Don't forget that God put Adam and Eve in the Garden of Eden and told them what they could eat. If eating had nothing to do with their walk with Him, He probably would not have mentioned food. Make good choices! Each time you choose good healthy foods, you are choosing life, which is God's gift to you. He wants you to look great and feel great and you can if you keep in mind that your body is the temple of God and the fuel you put into it determines how it will operate and for how long.

2. *Avoid Refined Carbohydrates*

Much of America's soaring rates of obesity and related incidence of heart disease and stroke are caused by the huge amount of refined carbohydrates we eat. (The rest is from lack of exercise.) This comes primarily as white flour (in bread, crackers, pasta, tortillas, cakes, cookies, donuts, pastries, pretzels), potato (french fries and potato chips), and sugar, corn syrup, and other sweeteners. On average, we each eat thirty-three pounds more sugars per year than we did thirty years ago and sixty-four pounds more grains (mostly white flour). Of the 425 pounds of "vegetables" we eat, more than 100 pounds are french fries and potato chips! If you simply make an effort to avoid these products, and do nothing else, you will do wonders for your health. Let's make it really simple: always choose the side salad or the vegetable instead of the fries. Don't eat the rice unless it's brown, and switch to multigrain bread. None of this is a hardship! Diabetes is a hardship. Wheelchairs are a hardship. Good health is easy.

3. Be Fierce about Fruits and Vegetables

If you have a passive spirit when it comes to eating, then America's chain restaurants and food packagers are going to force a lot of cheap grains down your gullet. Vegetables are more expensive than grains, and they spoil, so they are inconvenient for food companies that want to maximize profits. That middle bun in the Big Mac is not there for your benefit! It's the absolute cheapest way of making the sandwich look bigger. The same goes for the basket of bread on your table in a restaurant—it's the quick, cheap way of filling you up. These cheap carbohydrates don't provide much nutrition, but they taste good, so if we don't make the effort to seek out fresh fruits and veggies, our bodies will happily eat themselves sick on fries, bread, and sugar. The best defense is a good offense, and I want you to be *offensive,* if that's what it takes to get something decent to put into your body. Choose your restaurants and your dinner menus by the vegetables. I love restaurants that offer several choices of steamed vegetables. Use fruit to nip hunger in the bud. It's impossible to gain weight or get unhealthy by eating too many fruits or vegetables—their water content and fiber prevent that—so eat them aggressively, and think of them as armor for your battle against the Twinkies of the world.

- Make sure you have at least one fruit or vegetable with *every* meal. (And no, ketchup is not a vegetable!)

- For hors d'oeuvres, serve raw vegetables (broccoli, carrot, tomato, peppers) with a healthy dip.
- Make fruit your snack of choice.
- I've been known to walk into fast-food restaurants armed with fruit, cottage cheese, and carrot sticks. If my family wants to eat in a burger place but I don't want to fight the temptation, I stop by a grocery store, buy my own healthy food, and bring it with me. Radical, but it works!

4. *Replace Saturated Fat and Trans-Fat with Unsaturated Fat*

The easiest way to make your risk of heart disease plunge is to eat less red meat, dairy, and processed foods made with hydrogenated oils, and eat more fish, poultry, olive oil, nuts, and avocados. This doesn't mean you can't have a steak once in a while, but it does mean you shouldn't eat butter with every meal.

- Eat fish twice a week for dinner.
- Eat turkey breast or tuna sandwiches instead of roast beef or ham.
- Avoid bacon and sausage.
- Use olive oil on bread and in dressings.
- Add nuts and avocados instead of excessive cheese to sandwiches and salads.

5. *Balance Your Plate*

Look at a typical American dinner plate, and what do you see? A huge pile of ribs dripping off the side, another huge mound of mashed potatoes, a mountainous roll, and a tiny portion of salad or cole slaw trying not to get pushed off the plate. You can eat all of these foods (and whatever else you most love to eat), you just need to change the ratio. That salad or other vegetable (or, gasp, *two* vegetables) should take up half your plate, while the meat and starch each get a quarter.

➤➤➤ TAKING ACTION ➤➤➤

"Be doers of the Word, and not hearers only."
(James 1:22)

Choose at least one action you can take to eat more healthy foods. Write it down, *commit to it,* and begin today.

Action: _____

➤ KEY 6 ➤

Water Your Life

You are two-thirds water, just as the earth is two-thirds water and one-third dry land. (And the saline content of your blood is amazingly close to that of seawater.) You, and all living creatures, must maintain that water content precisely. If it drops below normal, sickness appears. Water is so fundamental to our existence that the Bible even compares it to the Word of God. We water our bodies with natural water and our souls with the water of God's word.

> So that He might sanctify her, having cleansed her by the washing of water with the Word. That He might present the church to Himself in glorious splendor, without spot or wrinkle or any such things.
>
> Ephesians 5:26–27

Just as the water of God's word washes our souls of spiritual filth, so water bathes every one of your cells in life-supporting fluid. It's also the fluid *within* your cells. The water passages of your body are the way materials are transported to the cells and the way waste is removed from the cells, just as the waters of the United States were the main transportation routes before the automobile. Without water, energy can't get from your food to your muscles and brain, waste can't get cleansed, kidneys can't function, and the immune system can't circulate. You can't cool yourself, either; those little water droplets that get pushed out through the skin as sweat are your main means for dumping excess heat. You can lose a quart of water through sweat if you exercise hard for an hour. If you want your cells to function at their peak—and everything we do or think depends on the functioning of our cells—then you need to provide your body with enough water to do its job.

If we don't get the water we need, things get ugly. You can go on a hunger strike for a month and suffer no problems worse than a loose wardrobe, but go on a water strike for more than a day and the consequences are severe. Serious dehydration begins with nausea, dizziness, and confusion and leads to muscle cramps, kidney failure, and death.

Even low-grade dehydration has important consequences. When the water level in your body drops, your blood has more trouble getting fuel and other nutrients to your cells, so your energy level drops. Your brain can't run at full power, either. You may not even realize you're thirsty, but the evidence is there: fatigue, grumpiness, and weak concentration. If this sounds like you, every afternoon, then you are probably not getting enough water. And if you try to fix the fatigue with coffee or cola, it's even worse: you burn up your remaining energy much faster and are left more dehydrated by the coffee, which is a diuretic. You'd be surprised how many afternoon slumps can be solved by water.

Let your low-level dehydration go on for too long and you suffer more. Dry, itchy eyes, dry skin that doesn't "snap back" when pulled, constipation, and kidney stones. Other long-term effects can be even more insidious. A friend of mine had a father who was showing signs of Alzheimer's disease: confusion, forgetfulness, and so on. My friend is a man of prayer, and he asked God to show him how he might help his father. It came to him that his father never drank water! He claimed he didn't like the taste. So my friend convinced his dad to start drinking water, and sure enough the signs of Alzheimer's disappeared. This does not mean that water can cure Alzheimer's disease. It means that chronic dehydration can be one cause of Alzheimer's-like symptoms.

Don't rely on thirst to tell you when you need more water. Thirst isn't always reliable, especially in the elderly. You get used to feeling all sorts of ways, some of them bad. Don't get so used to being thirsty that you don't notice! An employee of mine switched from other drinks to water throughout the day and was amazed by how much better she felt. "If a person drinks more water, can it make her thirsty?" she asked. Once she started drinking water, she felt thirsty. Her body was crying out for more, more, more water! Give someone a taste of freedom, and he wants more. Give your thirsty body a taste of good, clean water, and suddenly it realizes what it's been missing, and the thirst alarm goes off.

Water and Weight Loss

Believe it or not, drinking water helps you tremendously with weight-loss goals. This is partly because of water's ability to increase metabolism, as I pointed out earlier. Drink more water and you will burn a few more calories per hour, regardless of exercise. Water also helps fill your stomach—temporarily. But that can make the difference if it slows down your eating and gives your body time to realize it's full before you overeat.

I suspect that the reason a lot of people need to snack throughout the day is dehydration, rather than low energy. Since mild dehydration registers as fatigue and poor concentration, rather than thirst, many people mistake the feeling for hunger. They believe they have "low blood sugar" and need a snack. They end up snacking throughout the day, or reaching for the coffee pot again and again, when all they really need is a tall glass of cold water to completely revive them.

But the biggest reason water is a weight-loss godsend is because when you drink water, you are *not* drinking the other stuff—sodas, shakes, sweetened iced tea or coffee, energy drinks, and so on. Americans drink more than 400 calories of beverages in an average day, and that adds up to more than forty pounds a year of extra weight.

I recently visited a relative of mine whom I hadn't seen in months. She looked great, and I asked if she'd lost weight. She had lost twenty-five pounds. "All I did was start drinking a lot of water," she said. Right there is the simplest diet you will ever see. No changes in meals or exercise at all; simply switch to water from caloric drinks and watch the pounds melt away. If you tend to drink more than a couple of sodas or juices a day, it can easily add up to twenty or thirty pounds a year. You'll never find an easier way to improve your health and your waistline than by cutting these unnecessary drinks out of your diet.

Simply switch to water from caloric drinks and watch the pounds melt away.

At first, this may seem difficult. Good water is delicious, but taste buds blunted by sugar have trouble appreciating it. If you are used to tasting sugar in every sip, it will feel like something's missing at first. Your taste buds will need some time to readjust. But readjust they will! After a few weeks, you will be on the other side of the fence: water will taste great, and those sugary drinks will taste awful. You'll wonder how you ever could have drunk anything so sweet. Water tastes so much more refreshing to me than anything else. I don't drink it simply because I know it's good for me. I drink it because I love it, and it makes me feel good.

How much water do you need? A well-known formula is to take your weight, divide by two, and get that many ounces of liquid a day. Eight ounces is a cup, so if you weigh 128 pounds, you should be getting eight cups of water a day. If you weigh 160 pounds, you should be getting ten cups. Not all this has to come from drinking water. Other liquids count, including the water you get in your fruits and vegetables.

What About Caffeine?

Years ago, I cut caffeine out of my life. That was one of the hardest things I've done. I loved my coffee. There was nothing I enjoyed more than getting up early and spending some quiet time with the Lord over a cup of fresh, hot coffee. But eventually I came to accept the fact that coffee was not agreeing with my system anymore. I did everything I could to hold on to caffeine! I gradually decreased the amount of regular coffee I drank and replaced it with decaf. It never tasted right, and still my system was upset. Because my body was so stressed, it was necessary for me to cut out caffeine entirely for a period of time. I went over to decaf. Coffee lost much of its luster for me.

But in the past few years, I've turned this around. I am healthier now and I learned that caffeine on its own is not necessarily a problem. Caffeinated drinks, like coffee and tea and soda, are simply low-grade stress in a cup. Caffeine makes all the classic changes happen in your body that occur in response to any physical or mental stress: the heartbeat quickens, breathing increases, senses sharpen, and your brain picks up speed. This feels good, as do lots of other gentle stressors, like exercise, amusement park rides, and even falling in love! As I'll explain in my chapter on stress, it's only when stress gets out of control in our lives that it becomes a problem and causes disease, sleeplessness, and premature aging. Our bodies are created to be able to handle a normal amount of stress but unfortunately, in twenty-first-century America, stress is out of control in most of our lives.

That's what happened to me. I was running myself ragged, my system was on stress-overdrive day and night, and coffee just added more fuel to the fire. So I cut it out. But once I made the lifestyle changes to reduce my stress to normal levels, I discovered to my great joy that I could drink a little coffee each day with no repercussions. I now enjoy a cup of cappuccino in the morning and another in the afternoon. It perks me up just when I need it, and I'm careful to avoid excess in this area.

You'll be pleased to hear that nutritionists give caffeine a clean bill of health. It causes no health problems at moderate dosages. (Earlier studies linked caffeine with a number of health problems, but it turned out that was because so many caffeine drinkers also smoked, and the smoking was the cause of the health problems.) Caffeine even helps reduce your chances of developing kidney stones, gallstones, and depression. Most amazingly of all, a major 2005 study found that coffee is far and away American's biggest source of antioxidants! Drinking many cups a day, however, causes the classic symptoms of high stress—sleeplessness, anxiety, shakes, and digestive problems—and may contribute to osteoporosis. It's also addictive; stopping cold turkey will give you a nasty headache. Stick to two or fewer cups per day and you'll have no worries.

Other Drinks

Anything you guzzle counts toward your liquid intake goals—but many come with a nasty and unnecessary caloric wallop. Here are the calories in some common convenience store offerings:

Grapefruit juice (16 oz)	280
Milk (16 oz)	220
Cola (16 oz)	200
Iced tea (16 oz)	160

Some of these drinks do have redeeming value. Fruit juices (if fresh and 100 percent juice) have vitamins in them. Milk has vitamins and protein. Skim milk is an excellent beverage; whole milk is very high in saturated fat. Sodas, sweetened teas, and "energy drinks" are just sugar water in disguise.

Fortunately, every convenience store and supermarket also has good bottled water for sale, and sparkling water for those who want to liven things up a bit. There are also diet drinks. These are calorie-free, and are a better bet than regular sodas or sweetened tea. If they help you get off the sugar addiction, then they are beneficial. But health concerns have been raised about some of the artificial sweeteners. The new generation seems to be safer, but no long-term studies on people have been done because the sweeteners are too new. And something seems fundamentally suspicious about introducing new man-made chemicals as food that no human body has ever encountered before. You will also never awaken your taste buds from their sugar-glazed stupor if you keep them hooked on diet soda. Personally, I stick to drinks with a long safety record: water, sparkling water, coffee, herbal tea, and an occasional fruit juice.

Five Ways to Stay Hydrated

1. Make It Taste Good

Lousy tap water is a serious impediment to drinking eight cups of water a day. This task shouldn't be torture for you, it should be pleasant and hassle-free. Do what you have to do to make your drinking something you look forward to; that's the only way you know you'll keep doing it. Some ideas:

- Put a filter on your tap
- Buy bottled water
- Squeeze a wedge of lemon or lime into every glass

- Make iced herbal tea
- Decaf coffee and tea are fine choices, though they don't taste great
- As a last resort, new lines of flavored waters are available that are ever-so-slightly sweetened. With only a handful of calories per cup, they make a good "bridge" in your transition from sweetened drinks to water.

2. Carry Water Everywhere

You can remind yourself to drink more water, but if it isn't on hand, you won't do it. Making sure it's always on hand will go a long way toward establishing this new habit. I carry water with me everywhere—business meetings, church, car trips, you name it. I am thirsty for water most of the time. Yet I drink water all day long. That's because drinking it makes me aware of how much better I feel when I'm fully hydrated, and my body becomes eager to stay that way. Keep bottles of water in your car, your home, and your office, so that you don't even have to think before reaching for it. And when you go to a restaurant and the waitress pours your glass of water, drink it! Why order another beverage you don't need?

When I am on the road ministering, I carry two water bottle holders with me—one silver and one gold! That way I can match any outfit, stay fashionable, and make sure I have water with me at all times.

3. Have Your Water Call You

If you find it hard to remind yourself to drink a glass of water every hour or two, let technology solve your problem: set your cell phone to ring every hour as a water reminder! That's one drastic answer to make sure your water isn't "out of sight, out of mind." Here are some more:

- Fill a pitcher with ice water in the morning, at home or work, wherever you'll spend your day, and keep it in front of you as a reminder to drink. You'll be able to tell if you're slipping throughout the day.
- Keep a water checklist each day. It's easy to lose track!
- Ritualize your water drinking. Tie it to specific times throughout the day as natural reminders. The easiest is probably your meals. Drink a glass of water at the beginning of each meal. You'll be assured of getting your water in, and will likely eat a little less as a bonus. First thing in the morning is another great time for a glass, to get the metabolism started. Right before bed is not so good, because it may prevent you from sleeping through the night.

4. Eat Fruit Every Day

Fruit can be eighty percent water or more, so if you eat several pieces of fruit a day (as you should), you get an extra glass of water. Some vegetables are also high in water content. You certainly can't expect to meet your entire fluid requirements through food, but it all counts.

5. Install Water Coolers

Studies have shown that if people see water coolers, they are more likely to get a drink of water than if they have to get one from the tap. The water cooler functions as a subtle suggestion and people trust that they'll get tasty water from it. If your office doesn't have a water cooler, suggest installing one. You'll improve the health of the entire office. They work surprisingly well at home, too.

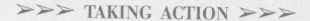

TAKING ACTION

"Be doers of the Word, and not hearers only."
(James 1:22)

Choose at least one action you can take to drink more water each day. Write it down, *commit to it,* and begin today.

Action: _____

➤ KEY 7 ➤

Mindful Eating

See if any of this sounds familiar:

Every time you get a snack out of the refrigerator for your children, you pop a little in your mouth. Half a piece of cheese, a slice of ham, or a spoonful of peanut butter.

You have no intention of eating the cake you bake, but you lick clean the batter bowl and the icing knife.

You get a muffin every day at Starbucks, but throw out half of it to "save calories."

You don't order dessert because you're on a diet, but you ask your husband for several bites of his.

You buy miniature candy bars, hide them, and eat just one a day, telling yourself that if they're miniature, they don't count.

Ring any bells? These are all bad habits I got into in the past through mindlessness. My conscious mind told myself that I ate responsibly, and if you looked at my three main meals, I did. But there was a lot of extra eating going on every day that I wasn't even aware of. Finishing off kids' leftovers. Sampling food while I cooked. Plundering my husband's desserts.

And those little candy bars! They were so small I figured they could be ignored. Each had only 100 calories, which doesn't seem like a lot, but I was eating one every single day. Take any food you eat every day, divide its calories by ten, and that is how many pounds of difference it makes in a year. That one bite-size candy bar was adding ten pounds a year! Once I realized that, I stopped right away. It wasn't worth it. Two seconds of pleasure for constant guilt and weight-gain.

Quality decisions must be made if we are to take charge of our bodies. I got rid of my bad food habits by making the commitment that every piece of food I put in my mouth would be a conscious decision. This is harder than it sounds. A shocking number of the calories we consume every day come independent of hunger. You know how it goes. The box of doughnuts or the birthday cake in the office. The cola or iced tea in the car while you drive. And the classic: when you watch TV at night, do you have "a little something" to keep your hands and mouth busy? Chips? Ice cream? Most of us do, even if it's a "virtuous" 100 calories of grapes.

Say you have titanium willpower and never consume a calorie while driving, at the office, or watching the tube. Are you off the hook for mindless eating? Not necessarily. "Seconds" could be your downfall. You clear your plate and automatically pile it up again, and if the serving bowls are on the table, it makes it even easier. If you are at a friend's or relative's house, you'll certainly be offered more—and it would be rude to refuse, wouldn't it? Many people consider seconds an automatic part of dinner and never stop to decide if they are still hungry or not.

And then there are restaurants. They don't offer you seconds; they do something even sneakier. They serve you such immense portions that your firsts are really firsts and seconds combined. Think about the size of the fast-food burgers we eat today, compared to the little cheeseburgers from when we were kids. Or the pasta meals we used to eat out, compared to, say, a certain chain restaurant's Cajun Chicken Pasta (1,190 calories, 56 grams of fat), which isn't even promoted as being large!

How did all this mindless eating come to pass? Are we all simply moral failures? Weaklings who can't control our gluttony?

I don't think so. We live in a unique time. Never before in human history has so much food been available so cheaply all the time. We stop for gas, and there is food. We go to work, and there is food. We shop at Wal-Mart or Costco, and there is food. There is food in our living rooms, our desk drawers, and our glove compartments. There is food on airplanes, in motels, and in conference rooms. There is food at the beach, the county fair, and the movie theater. There are vending machines in every school.

Satan specializes in temptations, and he is doing an awfully good job of putting temptations on every street corner. Most of us are strong enough to resist the occasional temptation, but few have the heroic willpower necessary to constantly resist. Part of the problem is that when we see food all around us, and other people eating it, our context changes. It seems normal to be munching on something just like everyone else. The girl at the fast-food counter asks us if we'd like to try an apple pie with that (and gets in trouble if she forgets). What a good idea!

My husband Dave and I were once on a business trip with a man who was thirty or forty pounds overweight and was forever on the prowl for what he could pop in his mouth next. He didn't have to go out of his way, either; food was offered to him throughout the day, and he always took it. The hotel put chocolates on the pillows in every room, and he instantly popped a few chocolates in his mouth and made sure to put the rest in his pockets. He practically emptied the bowl of peppermints in the lobby. Any time we passed a coffee shop he ducked in and emerged with some frothy beverage piled with chocolate and whipped cream. As far as I could tell, he gave little thought to any of this. He just saw the food and reached for it like an infant.

We must keep our guard up against this constant whisper to eat, eat, eat. As I explained in Key 1, few of us can do it by willpower alone, so we need to call on God to help us be mindful at all times. Mindful eating can be as important to looking and feeling great as eating the right foods.

What is mindful eating? It's simply being present—really present—whenever you choose to put food or drink in your mouth. It means asking yourself *Am I hungry? Do I really want this?* One of the most revealing questions to ask is *Does this even taste good?* It can be amazing how often you will say "no" about some food you were about to put in your mouth.

> Mindful eating means asking yourself Am I hungry? Do I really want this?

Does this taste good? can also save you from eating too much. Next time you eat, say, ice cream, be hyper aware of your experience. The first bite will knock your socks off. Few experiences in life can compete with the first bite of an ice-cream cone! The second bite's pretty good, too, though your brain doesn't do quite the same loop-de-loops. But notice what happens about halfway through that cone: you realize that you're hardly tasting the flavor at all. You've gotten used to it, and all that really registers by then is a general sweetness. But by then the *eat* instinct has kicked in and you are chowing down as fast as you can, ice-cream headache or not. At that point, a truly mindful eater throws the rest of the cone away. You've had your pleasure, you no longer taste much; it isn't good for you, so why eat it?

This doesn't just apply to ice cream. The flavor of any food starts to disappear after we get used to it. Develop the habit of leaving your plate half-full and you'll be much better off than automatically clearing your plate. I know there are hungry children in the world, but I don't see how stuffing my face and being overweight is going to help them. When you are in control of the portions, don't take more than you need. If you are in a restaurant where the portions are oversized, either split meals with another person or leave some on your plate.

Speaking of hunger, it's time we reconnected with it. If someone asked you, "Why do you eat?" you'd probably answer, "Because I'm hungry," yet it's amazing how often this isn't true. Most of us are clock-eaters: we have breakfast, lunch, and dinner every day, at pretty much the same time, regardless of hunger. Then there are those external cues, such as the beguiling smell of cinnamon buns in an airport kiosk that almost can't be denied. But they must be denied! Who is in charge, anyway? Your mind or the cinnamon bun? The Bible recommends in Romans 13:14 that we make no provisions for the flesh and put a stop to thinking about its cravings.

My husband grew up in a family that barely had enough to get by; nobody wasted food. As an adult he felt obligated to not only clean his plate but all of our children's plates too. As he got a bit older, he noticed he was gaining some weight and realized that he had to stop eating food just because it was there. Instead of eating too much so we don't waste any food, we should strive to prepare just what we know we are going to eat.

If you start to be truly present when you eat, and pay attention to how many items you are tempted to put into your mouth just because they are available, you will start detecting all the unconscious impulses your body has in reaction to food, and you'll learn to control them. You'll also become much better at knowing exactly what you've eaten at any given moment during a day, and you'll be able to plan ahead, which can dramatically improve your ability to eat sensibly.

For instance, as I write this it is noon and I know that so far today I have had:

1 cappuccino

$\frac{1}{3}$ of a lemon biscotti

1 small bowl of whole-grain cereal with fruit and 2% milk

2 rice crackers

1 nectarine

Approximately 20 ounces of water

I plan to eat later:

$\frac{1}{2}$ of a sirloin burger with $\frac{1}{4}$ of the bun

vegetables

cappuccino

For an evening snack I will probably eat one Weight Watchers fudge bar, which I really enjoy. It has only eighty calories. I will also probably eat one handful of some kind of salty crackers with the fudge bar, because I like the combination of salt and sweet. However, if we go to the movies I know I will want my half-a-box of popcorn, so I will skip the fudge bar and crackers after dinner.

Should I get hungry at any point during the day I will eat fruit.

For me, a particular challenge has been learning to politely refuse food when offered. When you are a preacher and spend a fair amount of time visiting other churches, after the service everybody invites you over to their house for a meal. For them, it is a special occasion to celebrate. For me, it becomes a daily problem.

Years ago, my husband Dave and I decided that when we go somewhere to minister, we won't eat with people after the service. If we do, we end up eating too many rich, celebratory meals with multiple courses. Everything tastes wonderful, of course, and we appreciate the sentiment, but now we politely refuse. That is a skill to learn in itself. You aren't being rude to refuse something you don't need. Don't do things out of obligation—especially with eating!

Don't Get Discouraged

Like anything else, mindful eating is a skill that takes practice to perfect. The more you do it, the better you will get, but there will be some bumps along the road. No matter how disciplined we are, we all backslide occasionally. Several months ago I started eating natural, freshly ground peanut butter, which I absolutely love. It's a wholesome food with a great combination of protein, healthy fats, and good taste—but it is rich in calories. I started eating just two natural graham crackers with *a little* peanut butter each night. Then the two became three, and eventually I was eating a dozen crackers with *a lot* of peanut butter, and drinking milk with them. After about six weeks I noticed that my clothes were too tight. To my dismay, I discovered I had gained six pounds, and I realized right away that the culprit was the peanut butter. What happened? I became mindless. I was not paying attention to how much I ate, so I mindlessly did more and more of it until my circumstances woke me up.

I did not get discouraged, however. I cut out the peanut butter entirely, and the six extra pounds went away. Now I only have the peanut butter occasionally, and when I do I limit myself to two crackers.

Another woman I know drank a glass of milk every night before bed for years. She didn't need that milk; she had just gotten used to it. When she finally made herself break that habit, she lost twelve pounds.

If you keep working at mindful eating, you will get better at it, and will backslide less. But you will still slip now and then, so don't beat yourself up when you do.

Five Ways to Be a Mindful Eater

1. *Pay Attention to How You Feel Afterward*
I used to think that a big plate of pasta was one of my favorite lunches. And I surely enjoyed it while I was eating it. But about twenty minutes later an overwhelming sleepiness would come

over me. I had no energy for work and felt downright grumpy. I wouldn't recover until much later in the afternoon. It took me *years* to connect this with the pasta. Now I know that eating pasta or other starches with little or no protein wrecks me for hours.

The same thing happened to me with popcorn. When I go to a movie, I love to eat popcorn and candy. It feels great when you're doing it, but eventually I noticed that after a popcorn-and-candy blowout, I felt awful the next day. Extremely tired and down. So I've learned to eat plenty of protein the day that I plan to go to a movie, to eat less overall and save some room, and to eat just half a small box of popcorn and maybe ten M&Ms. Then I enjoy myself and feel fine the next day.

How many of your "feeling bad sessions" are connected to bad food you ate earlier that day or the previous evening? It could be quite a few! Our days are too precious to waste feeling bad, so if you are caught in this trap, you need to take action. Food is not just about the immediate gratification when chip hits tongue; it's supposed to give you fuel, energy, and a sense of well-being throughout your days and life.

Junk food exists only because people don't sense the connection between what they eat and how they feel. Once you get good at being mindful of this, you'll be amazed at how it changes your eating habits. You'll actually feel drawn to salads and other healthy foods, because you'll come to associate them with the good feelings they give you. And chips and cookies may start to taste lousy as you instantly become aware of the lousy reaction your body has to them.

Sometimes my flesh craves a big, greasy hamburger with all the fixings. But I don't have to give in to that flesh. A minute of thinking about the whole experience—the immediate taste sensation, the grease, and the sick feeling afterward—helps me to realize that there is more overall pleasure in a turkey sandwich on whole-wheat bread.

2. Say Grace

Thanking God for the bounty on your table is the best way I know to immediately bring yourself into a more healthy relationship with your food. If you have a tendency to overeat, ask God to help you at this meal to stay in His perfect will. God wants you to enjoy what you eat, and true enjoyment does not mean eating so much that you spend the next few hours feeling sick and guilty. Realize that this meal is not the last one you will ever eat. There will be plenty of other meals in your life so thank God, enjoy your food, make good choices, and stop as soon as you feel full.

Another great trick for reminding yourself that food is about more than taste is to tell yourself that you are eating for two. Many women switch to healthier diets once they get pregnant. They may have been willing to shortchange themselves nutritionally, but not their babies! Well, you are also eating for two. Since your body is the temple of the Holy Spirit, and you keep yourself healthy so that God can act through you in the world, you can see how important it is to keep God's "vessel" healthy. Don't shortchange Him!

(And by the way, if you are pregnant, eat for two, not three or four! Don't use pregnancy as a license to pig out and assume all the weight will disappear after you give birth. It won't. Many women gain too much weight when they are pregnant, have difficulty losing it, and literally fight with their weight the remainder of their lives. Pregnant women should gain about thirty pounds by the time they deliver. Try to stay closely in touch with your hunger. You will be ravenous at times, and when you are, eat and enjoy it. But don't think you can eat, eat, eat all the time.)

3. Don't Multitask with Food

When you eat . . . eat. When you work . . . work. When you watch TV, don't get out the candy. You will enjoy your life much more if you do one thing at a time and give it your full attention. And when you are distracted by something like TV or work, you get cut off from your natural sensations and are much more likely to keep stuffing food in without even knowing it. Many people are so used to having food around that they come to think of it like they do background noise. If they are working at their desks and aren't snacking on a bag of jelly beans, something just feels wrong.

It's essential to break this habit. Hundreds or even thousands of calories a day can go in, and you have little pleasure to show for it. Make sure when you are eating you truly enjoy it, and stop if you don't. For instance, when I get popcorn at a movie theater, I admit I'm multitasking—hey, nobody's perfect!—but I only get a little, and I truly enjoy it. I'm *very aware* that I'm having popcorn (and I've saved room during the day for a specific amount). I don't just get popcorn because "that's what people do at the movies" and toss it mindlessly in my mouth while I watch. I also go to the movies rarely enough that the movie/popcorn connection is truly a treat for me.

4. Slow Down

As I explained in Key 5: Balanced Eating, it takes about twenty minutes for the food you eat to pass through your stomach and reach your small intestine, which detects the food and sends "all full" messages to the brain. But if you have the hi-power feedbag strapped on, by the time those messages get sent from the small intestine, it is too late; a lot more food is already in the pipeline, and you're painfully stuffed. Slow things down and you give your body more time to cut you off. Some tips:

- Chew your food well.
- Swallow one bite before reaching for another.
- Eat several small courses instead of one huge plateful.
- Have relaxed conversation with friends or family while you eat, but never discuss anything intense or upsetting.
- Have your salad first. By the time you get to the more calorie-dense main course, you won't be ravenous.
- Don't let yourself get too hungry. When we're starved, it's hard not to inhale our food.

5. Turn Off the "Bargain" Detector

We Americans have become incredibly savvy at getting good deals. The huge tub of nuts for $2 at Costco. The weekend in Cancun for $199. But when we start thinking like bargain shoppers about our food, we get into trouble. Hear me loud and clear: all-you-can-eat buffets and salad bars do you no favors! They plant the notion in your head that the more you eat for the same price, the better the deal. But once you eat beyond what you need, the only deal you receive is a cut rate on diabetes and cardiovascular disease. Restaurant portions are already usually more than you need, so all-you-can-eat is truly obscene. So is super-sizing your fast-food meals. I don't believe anyone feels a burning need for more food after consuming a regular burger and fries, so why order it, even if it's only an extra thirty-nine cents?

Dave and I often split meals at restaurants. With soup or salad, one entrée is usually plenty for the two of us, and it leaves us enough room to occasionally split a dessert. We get an affordable meal and dessert, too!

Buying large "family packs" can get you into trouble, too. If you eat a normal portion and freeze the rest of the package (or have a big family to feed), great. But if you end up eating more than you normally would, or digging the leftovers out of the fridge "before it goes bad," then the good deal isn't worth it. You are what you eat, and if "bigger is better" doesn't apply to you, then it doesn't apply to your food, either.

And don't fall for the classic mistake of buying sodas or juices instead of bottled water in convenience stores because "I can get water at home for free." Your choice is between a dollar's worth of health and weight loss or a dollar's worth of diabetes. It can feel frustrating to pay a dollar for water at a gas station when you can get it for free at home, but you're *not* at home. And if that bottled water saves you from consuming soda, juice, sweetened tea, or slushies you don't need, then that's one of the smartest dollars you'll ever spend.

➤➤➤ TAKING ACTION ➤➤➤

"Be doers of the Word, and not hearers only."
(James 1:22)

Choose at least one action you can take to eat more mindfully. Write it down, *commit to it*, and begin today.

Action: _____

➤ KEY 8 ➤

Curb Your Spiritual Hunger

There are some things in life that we can't control, and some of those things bring us pain. Illness or injury bring physical pain. Other people can say or do cruel things that cause us emotional pain. And sometimes it doesn't take people at all; circumstances can deal us a bad hand and cause a lot of pain and suffering. Not all of these events are necessarily traumatic. Lots of small little hurts in our lives can add up to a general state of sadness or low-grade despair. Sometimes the simple lack of stimulation from loved ones in our lives can contribute to boredom and loneliness, which can be some of the hardest emotional suffering to endure.

Wouldn't it be nice if we could control the people and circumstances in our lives and avoid pain entirely? It's a natural wish; nobody likes pain. Unfortunately, none of us have that control. We all have to live the life we have, and through a personal relationship with Jesus Christ we can enjoy our lives whether our circumstances suit us or not.

Even if we can't control all of our circumstances, one thing we do have control over is what we put in our bodies. And there's no denying that a lot of these things give us pleasure. Every time I pop a strawberry in my mouth, that's a little hit of pleasure. A cool drink on a hot day can be pure joy.

I am sure you don't need me to convince you of the dangers of smoking, or the terrible cost of addiction to drugs and alcohol. We're all aware that such substances are pleasure shortcuts. When you don't have inner contentment, it becomes all too easy to go for the quick rush of pleasure provided by these vices—even if such pleasure is short-lived and comes with the chronic pain, suffering, and illness of addiction.

But people are less aware that food can play the same role. If I feel down and I eat that strawberry, I feel better for a moment. Not long—the good sensation lasts only a fleeting instant after I swallow the strawberry—but fortunately there's another strawberry after that one. And another after that. And even if the strawberries run out and my depression returns, there's that pint of ice cream in the fridge for just such emergencies. When the ice cream is gone, there is the chocolate cake or the pie. When we turn to food for comfort, we establish a pattern that is unhealthy and even dangerous—and still leaves us without the comfort we seek.

Food addiction is easy, because food doesn't come with the same stigmas as cigarettes or drugs. Unlike these vices, food has a legitimate—even essential—role in health. Only when it slips into overuse does it become a problem. But it's so easy to get to that point! Food is reliable. Unlike spouses, friends, or great weather, it is *always* there. But that's the problem. Any time we feel spiritually empty, whether through sadness, depression, or boredom, it's easy to reach for food to fill that void. Soon, we mistake spiritual hunger for physical hunger, and food becomes the immediate answer to any drop in well-being.

You know where this leads. The more you try to treat your spiritual longing with food or other feel-good stimuli, the greater your soul's cry for spiritual nourishment will be. The greater your *dis-ease* will become.

Fortunately, there is another source of comfort that is always there when you need it. Unlike bad food or drugs, it doesn't leave you overweight, sick, or lethargic. It's even free. That something is God. He is called the "Father of sympathy and the God of every comfort, who consoles us in every trouble" (2 Corinthians 1:3–4).

When I hurt, I have learned to run to God first, instead of another person or substance. I'm not saying this is automatic. It took me years to get this straight, and I still sometimes have to remind myself that what I truly need is *spiritual* nourishment. But learning this habit will do more to keep your mind and body

> When I hurt, I have learned to run to God first, instead of another person or substance.

sound and your life on an even keel than anything I know. Your spirit needs nourishment just like your body does. Don't wait until you have a crisis in your life to start feeding it.

Today's Spiritual Famine

Today more people are spiritually malnourished than ever before. Too many elements of society distract people from their eternal souls and encourage them to concentrate on material life instead. People get caught up with making money to buy bigger homes and spiffier cars, or with following the latest trends. Families are less likely to live close together, removing another spiritual support. Time for church and religious matters, or even for spending quiet time in nature, is pushed aside by busy schedules and entertainment. The quiet voice of God is drowned out by the constant drone of the TV set.

Caught up in this lifestyle, many people mistake the void they feel inside for physical hunger. They were never taught to recognize spiritual hunger, or what to do about it if they do recognize it. Since they don't know what to do about the pain and loneliness, they reach for the quickest fix they know: food, drugs, alcohol, or other material pleasures.

Even those who do know better and make the effort to be good Christians can get swept up in this spiritual famine, because so many entertainment venues are closed to us. There are not many parties we can attend, not many movies we can watch without feeling debased. I even had to leave an opera once because of the vulgar language being used on stage. I find that so frustrating! It seems that Satan is out to ruin everything in this world that God's people enjoy. His goal is that we become so bored that we eat ourselves to death or do other equally destructive things. We assume food is one of the few entertainments open to us that is free from sin, only to fall into the trap of gluttony, which God's word definitely condemns. God wants us to enjoy what we eat, but He does not want us to eat ourselves into disease or early death.

I'm certainly not immune to these temptations. I live my daily life in the spiritual realm, but that can leave me just as exhausted as if I was digging ditches all day. We in the ministry have made the commitment to lay down our lives to serve others, and are glad to do so, but that doesn't mean it automatically fills us with excitement every single day! I have to stick really close to God to keep my spirit nourished and to draw my enthusiasm from Him.

This may sound like a pretty grim picture. "If living a satisfied life in the Spirit is something that even Joyce or others in full-time ministry struggle with, how can the rest of us possibly combat such a state of affairs?" But don't despair. When you focus on the one person you can control—you!—it is doable. Take a good, hard look inside and decide whether your eating—or other addictions—comes from a spiritual hunger. Some of the classic signs are:

- You binge. Or binge and purge. This is a sure sign that you aren't eating from physical hunger.
- You make deals with God about your addiction ("Just let me enjoy this one cigarette, and I won't have any tomorrow," or "I'm going to eat this box of cookies now, but I promise to run three miles this evening") but you make no attempt to listen to His answer, or to engage in any real spiritual dialog.
- You lie to yourself or others about how much you have eaten that day, or keep food hidden and wait to eat it until no one is around.
- Your immediate reaction to stress is to think about food or begin snacking on whatever is near.
- Your weight-gain or substance abuse started after the loss of a loved one, something you perceived as a personal failure, the end of a relationship, or losing a job.

- You often find yourself at a loss for what to do in the evenings, and end up eating by default.
- You feel that no activities are quite complete unless they are accompanied by food.
- You end up feeling sadder after eating than when you started.

Why Bother?

So you've identified a lack of spiritual nourishment in your life. Why fix it? What's it going to give you, and how could it possibly help you kick your food or substance addiction?

If you have a rich spiritual life, you'll already be satisfied with the moment, the day, the year, and won't feel the need to "supplement" your moment with food. We all have these moments at times. You wander through a summer field of fireflies and suddenly feel still and awed at the beauty of it all. You hold your new son or grandson on your lap and feel a great spiritual bond of love all around you. You're sitting in a pew Sunday morning and the light comes through the stained glass and fills your heart with joy. The moment is complete in itself. You don't think, "My heart is full of joy and boy do I wish I had a slice of chocolate cake in my hand!" You can know the complete fulfillment of spiritual nourishment, and know that if you can experience it regularly, you'll have no problem eating and drinking only what you need.

In fact, we should all feel those transcendent moments more often than we do. I believe they are essential to physical, emotional, and spiritual health. And I think we spend too little time trying to achieve them and too much time meditating on our problems. Whether it's in therapy, at home, or with friends over coffee, if we stew in our own problems all the time, they are only going to be that much more with us. Get your mind off the problems, and spend more time meditating on the one true solution—God's love.

Our problems in life—and there will be problems—should drive us to God, not away from Him. Jonah tried running from his duty to the Lord by sailing to a remote destination, and look what happened to him! Don't follow Jonah's path. Run to God! He won't just help you find the solutions to your spiritual hunger, He *is* the solution!

Five Ways to Nourish Your Spirit

1. Stop Lying

The first step to receive God's love and true fulfillment is to stop denying to yourself (or others) that your problem is a spiritual one. You can't lie to God anyway, so why bother deceiving yourself? For years I was addicted to cigarettes, but I told myself that I kept smoking to stay thin; I didn't admit to myself that I had a spiritual weakness in that area. Truth is the way to spiritual fulfillment, and now is the time to start. If you need to, admit to yourself that your spirit is not getting what it needs from life. Once you do that, God will show you how to change that.

Who are you? What are your core values? Do the things in your life—the people, your job, and so on—support those values, or do they keep you separated from your true self? Try to identify the sources of the emptiness that drives you to eat (or smoke, or drink, or overwork); what imbalances are these creating in your life? What can you do to start filling those empty areas with activities or people that will help feed your spirit and connect you with God?

While you're being truthful with yourself, start being truthful in all the other areas of your life, too. Small untruths have a way of multiplying, and soon we are compromising in many areas. Not only does this make life harder in the long run, but it also makes it very difficult to have a genuine relationship with God. Sinning against your own conscience (doing things that you know are wrong) is one of the greatest sources of depression and discontent.

2. Ask

God loves you very much and wants to help you, but you need to ask Him to. A man told me recently that when he feels overwhelmed, he lifts up one hand toward heaven and says, "Come get me, Jesus." God hears the faintest cry of your heart, so stop trying to do everything on your own and ask Him for help.

The next time you are tempted to eat because you're upset or sad, say "no" out loud. Then go sit quietly for a moment and ask God to help you in your situation. You'll be amazed at how much of a difference asking makes. More often than not, you'll find that you suddenly have the strength to resist the temptation. But you have to *really* ask; you can't just tell yourself that you're open to God's help.

You may not think that God cares about something as simple

as your health, but He does. He cares about everything that concerns you—the big as well as the small. He wants you healthy, and He is willing to help, if you'll just let Him. Don't pray to Him to simply break your addiction; instead, pray to Him to help you find the spiritual strength to make the life-style changes that will make the bad symptoms disappear. God's grace is always available to partner with our choice. As we choose to do what is right and lean on Him to give us strength, His power enables us to follow through and experience victory.

Prayer and meditation on God's word is an excellent practice to nourish your spirit. It is spiritual food; feed your spirit regularly and you will be healthy and strong inside and out.

Studying God's word, or silent or verbal prayer, are traditional methods of making contact with God, but other activities can also make you receptive to His nourishing love. Read something that encourages you and gives you hope. Keep a gratitude journal where you list the good things that happened to you that day (and there are good things in *every* day).

3. Crowd Out the Bad Habits

Bad habits need room to operate. Not much—they're pretty clever—but there are situations where they can't get a foothold. If you have a job as an acrobat, you will have a hard time snacking mindlessly while you work. If you spend your evenings at a health club, good luck sneaking a cigarette in. One good strategy for keeping your bad habits at bay is to recognize what your temptations are, and then set up your life in such a way that they have no room to operate. Fill your life with so many positive, spiritually reaffirming things that there's no room for anything else. If you are tempted to snack in the evening, then don't keep unhealthy snacks in the house. If you tend to overeat when bored, then be sure you have something fruitful to put your time into.

Choose activities that help to fill that space inside you, your "God-space," with the feelings of love and completeness you are looking for. Instead of spending the weekend watching TV, visit a friend or relative you have not seen in a long time or go to a Christian conference. As God says, "Don't link up with those who will pollute you. I want you all for myself" (2 Corinthians 6:17, The Message). Another good way to spend time is helping someone else in need.

Exercise is a terrific way to fill time with healthy activity that leaves your spirit high and your body recharged. Read my chapter on exercise to learn all the benefits it gives you.

What other activities can replace some of your current unfulfilling pastimes? What friends do you have who you know are good at encouraging your new health commitment? Call them up and plan some dates. For example, my youngest daughter is very interested in staying healthy. She reads about nutrition, exercise, and good health principles all the time. Anytime I need a little extra encouragement to stay on the right path, I simply ask her what she has learned lately. She always has plenty of things to share that challenges me to keep on keeping on!

4. Support Programs
Breaking the habit of anesthetizing your spiritual hunger with food or other substances is a tough act, no question about it. Many people find the road easier if they have the support of a

group of people who have been there, can identify with how hard it is, and are trying to walk the same path. There are several good programs available throughout the country to help people break their addictions. They teach people to admit that they are powerless over the addiction, to believe that only God can restore them to sanity, and to make a decision to turn their will and life over to His care. Not everyone is comfortable finding their spiritual nourishment through groups, but many who were at first skeptical have found success this way.

5. Give It Some Time

Don't commit and make the decision to nourish your spirit, struggle through two days of no snacking and trying to remember to celebrate the moment, and then call me up and say, "Joyce! It doesn't work! Too hard!" These things take time. Don't plan on instant success.

When you first separate from a destructive behavior, you will actually feel like there is a void in your life. You've become so used to the wrong behavior being a part of your daily existence that, like having an abusive husband, you don't quite feel like yourself once it's gone, even if you know you're better off.

Don't worry. Change is always rough at first. As you've probably heard, it takes about thirty days to break a habit. So much of what you do isn't conscious but patterns scratched into your nerves and muscles and neurons (like catching a ball or signing your name), and it takes a few weeks to undo those patterns in your body.

However long it takes, the trick is to not put any pressure on yourself in those first weeks. Commit fiercely to success, but love yourself no matter what happens. You will have some slips, but you will have more successes. If you maintain faith in yourself and in God's guidance, suddenly a day will come, many weeks later, when you realize that things are coming much more easily to you. You no longer have to try so hard consciously. You have curbed your spiritual hunger at last and broken the addictive cycle in your life.

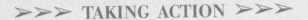 TAKING ACTION

"Be doers of the Word, and not hearers only."
(James 1:22)

Choose at least one action you can take to nourish your spirit. Write it down, *commit to it,* and begin today.

Action: _____

➤ KEY 9 ➤

De-Stress

There's a dangerous drug out there. Here's what just a little bit of it will do to you:

It sends your heart into overdrive, pounding at four times its natural rate. Same thing for your lungs. It constricts your blood vessels and raises your blood pressure to dangerous levels. It dries up your mouth and shuts down your stomach and intestines. It drains the blood from your face and skin. It scrambles your immune system. It wrecks your sleep, turns off sexual interest and reproductive capability, slows healing, and increases your risk of periodontal disease, skin disease, and autoimmune diseases. It turns off short-term memory and rational thought. It actually shrinks part of your brain. It even makes you overeat.

Sounds like bad news, doesn't it? I bet you'd go out of your way to steer clear of this drug. Yet you give yourself doses of it every day. I was addicted for years. The drug is cortisol, the most famous of the *glucocorticoids*. The glucocorticoids are stress drugs. And your body makes them daily.

When we say "I've had a stressful day" or "I'm stressed out," we mean that we can't relax. Things come up during the day, or carry over from previous days, that we must deal with. If there are enough things, or if they go unresolved, then there is no escape, no place to relax, and we are "stressed out."

Stress is the opposite of relaxation. Physically, it is your body gearing up to tackle whatever situation has arisen. And it does this by sending stress hormones in all directions. Out of your brain comes adrenaline (called *epinephrine* by scientists) and related hormones, and out of your adrenal glands come cortisol and the other glucocorticoids. Hormones are messengers that rush through the body, telling all your systems—your heart, muscles, skin, and so on—what to do. In this case, the message is *get ready for action.* We're all familiar with this as the "fight or flight" response.

In itself, that isn't a bad thing. Something urgent comes up, and your body instantly raises your systems to high alert to engage the situation. Then, once things calm down, you switch back to relax mode. This is a great system if you have to save a child from a burning building or run from a hungry bear. You get hyper-alert, super-quick, and you rescue the child, or leave the bear back at the Yellowstone campground. After a few minutes, your heartbeat comes down and life goes on. You get hungry and have a snack to make up for the energy you used racing through those flames.

You will be glad you have this system the next time you're faced with an emergency. The problem is not our bodies. The problem is our lives. Our bodies were not designed for twenty-first-century living, where mentally stressful moments are the norm, not the exception. All the changes that cortisol and the other stress hormones cause in our bodies help a lot in the short term, but can make us very, very sick—even kill us—if they happen every day. And if you lead a typical modern life, they happen not just every day but every hour. Ask yourself whether or not you have high stress levels. If the answer is yes, I urge you to read on—your life may depend on it.

What Happens to Us Under Stress?

To understand why we have the physical reaction to stress that we do—and why our bodies have our best interest in mind in doing so—we need to keep in mind how much our lives have changed from those of our ancestors. Most societies were centered around agricultural communities. People's main concerns were growing crops, raising livestock or fishing, and protecting their communities. The days were ruled by the slow rhythms of the seasons. Life was low-stress—except when it wasn't. Every now and then a war came along, or a flood or other natural disaster, or some other life-threatening event, and people were required to act fast. But it was not the norm.

Until recently, stressful events almost always required a physical response. Battling an invader, swimming for your life in a flood, or running from that bear. And all the changes that stress causes in our body make perfect sense if the goal is to survive the next few minutes.

Say the event is a forty-day flood. Suddenly you find yourself carried along, trying to stay afloat. At a signal from your brain, adrenaline and cortisol flood your body, and everything starts to change. Your breathing quadruples, pushing extra oxygen into your blood, and your heart races, sending the oxygen-rich blood to your muscles for power. That's why, under intense stress, we get faster and stronger. We've all heard stories of mothers who were able to lift a car off their trapped children, and there is some truth there.

That's not all. Stress makes our senses sharper too. Eyes dilate and hearing picks up. Very useful if you're struggling to keep your head above water in that flood and are desperately searching for a log to grab.

Your immune system changes, too. Your white blood cells stop working on long-term projects like slowly patrolling your body for cancer cells and instead rush to your skin and lymph nodes, ready to kill any germs that enter your body—which makes sense since stressful events are when you tend to get cut, stabbed, or bitten.

Your ability to feel pain goes down. We've all experienced the injury suffered during sports or while running from something that doesn't really get noticed until afterward, when we're back home and resting, and then it *really* hurts. Again, this is a great system, because drifting along in that flood, looking for an escape, is not the time to think about how much it hurt banging your shin on that underwater rock.

You even lose the ability to learn and think rationally. This may seem strange, but those qualities can indeed get in the way. Instead of spending time trying to figure out how many inches of rain you've had in the past forty days, you need to concentrate on instinctive thought—paddle, breathe, grab that overhanging branch.

Taken together, these physiological changes got our ancestors through many a scrape. When it comes to life-and-death struggle, you couldn't ask for a better coping mechanism. It seems almost magical, this ability to instantly increase our physical capabilities. It's as if you had a button in your Honda Civic that instantly turned it into a Ferrari when needed. The question is, if you have such a button, why not be a Ferrari all the time?

The answer is that all these increases in our short-term survival skills come at a cost. As I've discussed in previous chapters, your body has a set amount of energy, which comes from the food you've eaten and stored in your muscles and fat cells. When you operate as a Ferrari, you burn through that energy incredibly quickly. And in order to channel so much of your energy into your muscles and the other survival tools, you have to shut down all inessential systems.

When the issue at hand is not drowning, or escaping a wild animal, or fighting off an attacker, "inessential" means anything that won't help you do that, because if you don't survive the threat, nothing else will matter anyway. Reproduction goes right away—that's a *very* long-term project. Digestion shuts down, too. The food in your stomach might provide useful energy in a few hours, but you don't have that long, and besides, the blood used in your stomach and intestines for digestion is needed in your muscles right away. You lose your appetite too, of course. No use when dog-paddling down that swollen river to be thinking, "Gosh, a brownie would really hit the spot right now."

Your immune system doesn't shut down, but it does change goals. A big part of what it does is work through the lymph system, filtering out bacteria and damaged cells. Cells malfunction all the time, and your immune system is in charge of catching them before they turn into cancer. But when cortisol comes screaming through the body, sounding the alarm, the immune system drops such mundane tasks and rushes off to the front lines to guard against any invading germs.

In your brain, higher thought gets turned off, so you can concentrate on survival decisions.

A good way to think of it is to picture yourself as a country. You get attacked by terrorists and instantly go into high-stress mode. You ratchet up the military to be ready for any attacker, and you expand your intelligence operatives and spy satellites to report exactly what is going on out there. You post new immigration officers to make sure no new terrorists slip into the country. To pay for all this, you temporarily cut funding for education, higher learning, health care, and road maintenance.

This makes perfect sense short-term. If you get destroyed, road construction and education aren't going to matter. Once you've ascertained that you're safe, you can cut back the military and CIA and return the domestic programs to their previous level.

But if you get caught in a situation where you are constantly under attack from terrorists or foreign powers—or if you worry about it constantly—then you are in trouble. You keep pouring money into your defense budget, at the expense of all your other programs, and soon your roads are a shambles, your children aren't learning, and your people are sick. Instead of succumbing to a foreign threat, you break down internally.

That's what happens when you live in a constant state of stress. Cortisol, adrenaline, and the other stress hormones do a fantastic job of raising your game and getting you through a tense few minutes. Then you go back to relaxing for a few months until the next angry bear comes along. For most of human history, that's how it's been.

But it isn't that way anymore. Today, we experience stress on a daily basis, and unless you're a park ranger, it isn't usually the angry-bear variety. Today, the standard stresses include work pressure, financial worry, family conflict, social commitments, and even the daily grind of traffic jams and sporting events. Watching the St. Louis Cardinals lose the World Series is very stressful for some! Anything that gives you a rise, that increases your heart rate and breathing rate, is stress. Unfortunately, our bodies aren't designed for nonstop activity, traffic jams, and constant financial stress. They respond to these events, and all other nonphysical stress, with the exact same stress hormones.

When this happens most days, as it does for many of us, we start to break down internally, just like the country that's been on Code Orange for too many years. Occasional stress is healthy, even stimulating. However chronic stress doesn't allow the body to recover, and slowly kills it. Let's take a look at the different diseases caused or made worse by stress.

A Guide to Stress-Related Disease

Cardiovascular Disease

Perhaps the most important change that stress makes on your body is to increase the rate at which blood is pumped through it. That's the only way to get fuel—glucose and oxygen—to your muscles where it's needed (or where your body assumes it's needed, though it doesn't help much in a traffic jam). To do this, your heart beats faster, and your blood vessels constrict to force the blood through them faster. This means your blood pressure goes through the roof during stress. That is fine if it happens only occasionally, like during exercise. But if you are stressed all the time, then that elevated number *is* your blood pressure. Not good.

High blood pressure increases the pounding on the walls of your blood vessels (especially the Y's where a blood vessel branches into two). As I explained earlier, as soon as the cells that make up those walls get loosened up, material in your blood can get under them and stick to the wall, forming a blockage. Such blockages are the cause of heart attacks and strokes. No surprise, then, that people with heart disease are *four times* as likely to have heart attacks if they also suffer from high stress.

Diabetes

Stress is probably as big a factor in diabetes as diet is, and if we think about what happens during stress, it's easy to see why. When your body gets the alarm from your stress hormones, it wants to provide as much fuel as possible to your muscles. Increasing your breathing and heart rate is part of the answer. But your heart just circulates things; it doesn't provide the fuel. Where does the fuel come from? From your fat reserves. Adrenaline signals your fat cells to send their fat into your blood stream, where it can be converted into glucose for your muscles as needed. Your body tries to keep as much fat and glucose in your blood as possible during stress. To do this, it overrides your insulin, which is trying to force the fat and glucose into storage or muscle tissue. (The only places it doesn't override the insulin are muscles being used right then, which need all the glucose they can get.) Since insulin-resistance is the main problem for diabetics, stress makes it much worse.

Compounding the problem, your blood gets thicker during stress. Extra platelets get added to your blood, which are what make it clot. Blood that clots easily is what you want if your stomach is about to get sliced open by a sword or a bear claw, but not if you have diabetes or heart disease, because it is more likely to create blockages.

Now, take a moment to consider the overall impact of stress on your cardiovascular system. You've got thick, syrupy blood that is likely to clot pushing through your pounding heart and narrowed blood vessels with excessive force. If that isn't enough to get you on a stress-reduction regimen immediately, the rest of this section will.

Weight Gain

Earlier I said that stress suppresses appetite. The actual story is more complicated. During the first few minutes of stress, the adrenaline from your brain does indeed suppress hunger. That's the last thing you need to worry about until you've dealt with the stressor. But the cortisol from your adrenal glands actually stimulates appetite, and it takes longer than the adrenaline to circulate through your body and get removed from your body. It can still be there hours later. Cortisol's job is to take over after you have dealt with the immediate threat. It keeps your muscles and senses on high alert for a while, because that threat might still be around, and it tells you to *eat*. Since you probably expended a lot of energy in fight or flight, you now need to fuel up to be ready for the next emergency. Cortisol makes you ravenous, and it makes fat storage extra easy—especially around the abdomen. How helpful!

You probably know the scenario. You have a high-stress job, and for nine or more hours a day you run around like a headless chicken, hardly thinking about food. You may even skip lunch. No time! Then, finally, you trudge home at eight o'clock, pick up Chinese take-out, and practically inhale the little white cartons. The stress is gone (temporarily), you're unwinding, your cortisol is still going strong, and now it tells you to eat the whole chicken or pie and store those calories fast. That's why chronic stress is one of the main culprits in weight gain.

Don't confuse chronic stress with constant stress. Chronic stress happens every day, or almost every day, but doesn't have to be every minute of every day. Constant, unrelenting stress—such as a painful illness—doesn't cause weight gain because the adrenaline never goes away. Appetite is permanently suppressed. Such people tend to waste away instead.

Ulcers and Digestive Disorders

The slow process of converting food in your stomach to energy does not fall under the "emergency" category, so when faced with stress, your body shuts down digestion. Blood gets diverted from the stomach and small intestine to the heart and other muscles. Then, once the stress disappears, cortisol gets digestion cranked up again. If you have the kind of work or home life that involves brief stressful phone calls, meetings and presentations, interactions with colleagues or family, and hectic driving, then you have the classic on-off pattern of stress that breeds ulcers. Normally, your stomach wall is lined with a thick layer of mucus to protect it from the hydrochloric acid that breaks down food in the stomach. But when your digestion is frequently shut down by stress, your body can get out of step with making mucus to coat the stomach. Then the acid burns a hole in an unprotected spot on the stomach wall, and presto, you've got a nice, painful ulcer.

Your intestines also suffer under stress. While stress shuts down the stomach and small intestine, it actually speeds up the movement of the large intestine to unload any excess baggage in preparation for any "flight" you may have to do. When the stress goes away, this is reversed. But just like throwing your car back and forth between Drive and Reverse can mess up your transmission, regular on-and-off stress throws your intestines out of whack. They can spasm, causing (or aggravating) such conditions as colitis and irritable bowel syndrome (IBS).

Immunity

It's quite amazing how just experiencing stress can send your immune system into all sorts of cartwheels. When stress hits, you make extra white blood cells to fight infection. And cortisol pulls your existing white blood cells from their everyday ho-hum tasks like looking for cancer cells and sends them to the front lines to protect against infection from any puncture wounds you suffer during the stress. (Both fight and flight are more likely to result in cuts.) This is kind of like mobilizing the National Guard. After about a half-hour of stress, cortisol starts reducing the number of white blood cells you have in circulation. Why? If you keep those National Guard white blood cells on Code Orange, racing around the body looking for enemies and there aren't any enemies, eventually they start mistaking your *own cells* for enemies and attacking them. This is what's called an autoimmune disease—your own immune system at-tacks you. Some autoimmune diseases are Crohn's disease, Graves' disease, rheumatoid arthritis, MS, lupus, and psoriasis. So cortisol just tries to do its job by reducing the number of white blood cells.

But there's a problem. If your stress goes on for a while, corti-sol keeps reducing your white blood cells, until your immune system is depleted. Suddenly you are more likely to catch colds and other diseases.

As with so many other systems, a bit of stress isn't bad for your immune system. You get a quick lift and are less likely to get infections or colds during the initial minutes of stress. But soon, your white blood cell count starts to fall, and it keeps on falling the longer the stress goes on. Chronic stress greatly increases your risk of illness.

General Aging

We've all seen what happens to people who suffer through years of stress. Their hair turns gray. Their skin goes sallow and wrinkly. Everything from their eyes to their muscle tone just doesn't look right. By now, you should understand why. Corti-sol tells the body to drop all long-term projects and put all its resources into short-term survival. One of the longest-term projects is the general cell repair that goes on all the time and helps keep us young. Your body uses the protein in your diet to repair these cells, as well as the DNA in the cells. Under chronic stress, your body stops repairing its cells, and instead uses the protein as an extra source of fuel for "fight or flight." All main-tenance projects cease. That explains why people undergoing long-term stress look run down. They are breaking down on a cellular level.

Other Conditions

Think of anything bad that can happen to the body and stress will intensify it. Stress causes depression by throwing off your serotonin levels. It makes your muscles tense (which is useful if you are preparing for fight or flight), which leads to everything from back pain to migraines (caused by tense head muscles). It turns off higher brain functions and memory (to let you concentrate on quick, instinctive reactions to the stress), and chronic stress actually *shrinks* your hippocampus, the part of the brain that houses memory. It increases periodontal disease (your immune system doesn't fight as well against the germs that cause the disease), it slows growth in children, and inhibits reproduction in both women and men.

One obvious effect of stress is that it makes it difficult to sleep. Sleep is pretty much the opposite of stress. To sleep, you must relax, and you can't relax with all that cortisol racing through your blood and accelerating your heart rate and lungs. But lack of sleep in itself causes many of the same conditions as stress, including depression, accelerated aging, poor memory, low immune function, and weight gain. So you get a vicious circle of stress causing poor sleep, and poor sleep causing more stress. Simply feeling unhealthy is stressful, meaning all of the conditions caused by stress tend to reinforce it.

Time to get yourself out of that vicious circle! Our society is so supercharged and fast-paced that stress is guaranteed unless you put your foot down and refuse to live in the fast lane all the time. Today, if you are to live without dangerous stress loads, you must make the choice. You need a plan, and you need to know what to do. Here are some ideas to get you started.

5 Ways to De-Stress Yourself

This has been a long chapter—purposefully so. I find that people all nod their heads and give lip service to the idea that stress is bad and should be reduced in their lives, but they don't do a thing about it. It's too easy to stick with the status quo and stay under the gun of a stressful lifestyle. So I hope my explanations in this chapter make it very clear to you that stress is not an inconvenience. Stress is deadly. You *cannot* lead a full and righteous life if stress is breaking your spirit.

> *Stress is deadly. You cannot lead a full and righteous life if stress is breaking your spirit.*

I know of what I speak. For years, I was ruined by stress. I was sick and extremely tired all the time. I had headaches, back problems, hormone imbalances, cancer, and high blood pressure. I had a hysterectomy which I probably didn't even need. I worried a lot and tried to solve too many things. My schedule was insane and my mind never stopped churning. I did so much every day and worked so late every night that I could not get my system to calm down enough to sleep properly. I got emotionally upset regularly. Most of the time it was about my schedule, yet I was the one setting that schedule, so I had no one else to blame. Only I could change it, but it took years of misery to get me to the point of being willing to do so.

When I get through ministering at a conference, I'm tired,

physically, mentally, and emotionally. By the time I leave, I have given so much to others that there isn't much left. I finally learned that after a conference, I need to take some time to relax, do something I enjoy, get rid of my stress, and recharge my batteries. If I don't, I'm in trouble.

For years, I would come away from a series of meetings where the Spirit of God had been moving in great power. Then I would get home and have a bad attitude. I would get mad at Dave for going golfing and having fun while I was at home feeling lousy. I would feel sorry for myself, get angry, and take it out on others.

Now, after a conference, I take some time to eliminate stress. I might do it by treating myself and going shopping. Yes, shopping can be an excellent stress-reduction technique—if you love to do it, can relax while doing it, and don't get financially stressed while doing it. Or I might treat myself to a good clean movie. Often, I'll get a massage. Whatever it is, I know I won't be going back to work until I've eliminated the stress of responsibilities at the conference.

That's just one example from my life. I can think of many others, and I'm sure you already know of ways that work for you—though whether you actually do them is another matter. Now that you know how sick stress can make you, the next time you feel your body start to work itself into a frenzy, I hope you'll try something that you think will relieve it. The following are some of the classic tried-and-true methods.

1. Social Support

Studies show that social isolation leads to elevated cortisol levels. We are social beings, and hanging around with others is one of the best ways to make us feel good and relaxed. Various social outlets are right for different people; just make sure that you have *some*. My suggestions:

- **Family.** Sometimes family can be a great way to unwind (though sometimes it can be a significant source of stress!).
- **Church.** I've already mentioned that people who go to church weekly live much longer. They feel more secure and more loved and have lower cortisol levels to show for it.
- **Counseling.** If you don't have anyone else to talk to, being able to unload to a counselor can clear some mental space in your head and reduce stress.
- **Groups and Clubs.** Social groups of all kinds—book groups, walking groups, knitting clubs, Bible study groups, even groups of friends that simply meet for dinner once a week—are all shown to reduce stress.

2. *Shrug Therapy*

There are some things you can control in life—your choice of job, who your friends are, your coffee intake and late nights. There are others you can't—what other people say and do, the fluctuations of the stock market, the flat tire you got this morning. How you react to things you can't control helps determine your stress level and quality of health. People who regularly get upset over small things suffer in many ways. People who shrug them off do a lot better. The Bible calls it "casting your care."

Shrugging doesn't mean indifference; it simply means acknowledging that there is nothing you can do to change things at that particular moment. The flat tire has already happened; dealing with it by calling AAA makes sense, throwing a tantrum and kicking it doesn't. Don't be fooled by the "steam-engine" theory of the body. When psychology first became a science, steam engines were the dominant form of machine, so that's the model psychologists came up with for the brain. We build up pressure inside, and then have to "blow off steam" or we'll explode. But there's no evidence that the body works like that. Reacting with anger simply cranks up your whole system and raises your cortisol. So does silently simmering with anger.

The low-stress approach is to shrug things off. Life happens. God works in mysterious ways. If you trust Him to work things out, you'll navigate the dips of life with barely a blip in cortisol levels.

I spend time ministering in India and Africa, and I'm confronted with the terrible poverty and hunger I see there. I care very deeply for these people and do everything I can to alleviate it, but I realize I am only one person and can only make my contribution. I can let it burn me up and shake my fist at the unfairness of it all, but what does that accomplish, other than make me sick and possibly render me unable to do anything? I do what I can, but I don't get upset about what is beyond my control. Do your best, pray, and God will do the rest!

Control is a big issue. When people have control over a situation, they have much lower cortisol levels than when they don't. Responsibility is another issue. The more responsibility you feel for a given situation, the higher your cortisol. That's why you should run from any situation with that deadly combination of low control and high responsibility. For example, let's say you work at a restaurant and the computer system goes down. There is nothing you can do about it, in fact you don't even understand how the system works, yet you have a room full of hungry people and you are responsible for getting them some food. High-stress situation! You get all the blame, but have no authority to change things or take action that could have prevented the situation. There are situations you can't control, which is fine; just don't take responsibility for them. And when you do take responsibility for something (which is often the right thing to do), make sure you also have enough authority to make decisions and control what happens.

3. Find Your Element—And Stay There

My husband, Dave, once did one of the wisest things I've seen. Before we entered full-time ministry he worked as an engineer. He was offered a promotion that included a pay raise and a lot of prestige. But he turned it down. At first I was angry with him. I thought he was making a big mistake. Didn't he want to climb the corporate ladder? Wasn't he the best person for the job? He explained that he had watched the other men in that position. They had to travel extensively, and they were constantly saddled with unreasonable deadlines that put them under tremendous stress. "That is not the way I want to live," Dave said. He chose the position that allowed him to stick to his core values—commitment to family, and comfort with self—rather than chasing corporate power so others would look up to him. Besides, why choose a higher paycheck if you just spend it on doctor bills to relieve your stress-induced illnesses? Job stress causes as much illness in this country as smoking and lack of exercise. Like those things, it kills.

We all want more money, and then we get it and find that it doesn't change the basic dynamics of our life much. Maybe we drive a fancier car, or eat in better restaurants, but we are still the same basic person, and our happiness level doesn't really increase. The most important foundations to long-term happiness are being in right relationship with God, good health, a loving home life, work that is satisfying and not overly stressful, and enough money that you don't worry about finances. Everything else is gravy.

It's natural to care what everyone else thinks of you, and to desire a position where everyone looks up to you. But there's surprisingly little satisfaction there. I believe there could be much more happiness and less stress in the world if people would take the time to figure out their natural element and stay there. When you get offered a new position, ask yourself why you want it. If it's just for prestige, don't take it. Money is an important consideration, and can make some things in life easier, but don't take *any* job purely for the money if it's going to make you less happy on a daily basis.

It's difficult to tell yourself, "I'm not good at that," but it's very liberating! Once you say it, and are at peace with it, judgment and pressure disappear. Then you can concentrate on the things you are good at.

You may be in a position that doesn't make you happy and you need to make a change. You may be proud of your position, but if it steals your health, get out as fast as you can! If your superiors constantly make you feel bad about yourself, either work it out with them or consider going somewhere else. Reduce your level of stress if it's too high. Your element is waiting for you out there somewhere; if you aren't in it, go find it now! Jesus came so that we may "have life, and have it to the full" (John 10:10, NIV). Do whatever you need to do to make sure you fully enjoy the life He has provided for you.

Sometimes saying "no" takes more courage than saying "yes." You can take this concept beyond the work arena. Removing all the things from your schedule that aren't bearing good fruit will greatly reduce your stress level and enable you to truly enjoy the things you choose to concentrate on.

4. Nutrition, Supplements, and Diet

What you physically put into your body has a huge impact on your stress level. The most obvious example is caffeine. Caffeine causes the body to release adrenaline and cortisol. A cup of coffee is a cup of stress—it speeds your breathing and heart rate, tenses your muscles, hones your senses, and so on. It's great as a short-term performance booster, but too many cups a day can leave you stressed-out, with all the classic symptoms: sleeplessness, inability to concentrate, irritability, and so on.

Nothing else has the immediate and obvious effect on stress that caffeine does, but nutrition can be very important in regulating your stress. A high-protein diet avoids the mood-thumping effect of surging and crashing blood sugar brought on by a high-carb diet. Nutritional supplements and vitamins are also important. By revving up your metabolism, stress causes you to burn through certain vitamins at a furious pace, particularly vitamin C and the B vitamins. If you are under heavy stress, make sure you get extra doses of these in your food or supplements. I know many doctors bad-mouth supplements, but I also know first-hand what a difference they have made for me.

One over-the-counter product that has helped me tremendously is a combination of *Magnolia officinalis* and *Phellodendron amurense*, two herbs with long medicinal histories. This product has been shown in studies to reduce cortisol levels and promote relaxation and restful sleep without sedation. I have taken it for a couple of years and my sleep has improved, my muscles are no longer tense, and I have more energy than ever.

On the other hand, I have recommended this to friends who were stressed out and it did nothing for them. Each person's system is different. You'll need to experiment to find the right nutritional supplements for you. As with many over-the-counter herbs, there are varying opinions about the safety and effectiveness of this product. While they have been safe for me, you should consult your physician before trying any herbal supplements.

5. Relaxation Techniques

Relaxation is not selfish. It is not slacking off. It's a way of recharging your batteries—physical, emotional, and spiritual—so that you can charge back into the fray at full-strength tomorrow. You will get more accomplished in your days, and live longer and healthier and enjoy it more, if you take the time to treat yourself right. There are thousands of possibilities for how to do this. Here are some of the favorites:

- **Play.** We all know children need to play. It's essential for their development of physical and social skills, and also a way to relieve tension. But adults need to play just as much as children, and for the same reasons. Grown men, in particular, have a need to play. I know this because my husband, Dave, will call up one of his friends and say, "Can you play today?" Now, I admit, he's talking about golf, but it's all the same. Play is a terrific way to relax, because you get the fun of creativity and challenge without the pressure, because there are no "repercussions" based on your performance. (If you feel pressure to do well in a sport, however, then it isn't really "play," and you don't get the benefits. Remember, being first at everything is highly overrated, whether in play or work.) Choose a play activity that is flat-out fun for you and that is a total distraction and escape from the rest of your life.

- **Laugh.** "A cheerful heart is good medicine," says the Bible (Proverbs 17:22, NIV), "but a crushed spirit dries up the bones." Laughing good-naturedly at yourself and at life's ups and downs is one of the best stress-reduction practices. Experiments have even shown that people told to smile during a study—whether they felt like it or not—felt better by the end of the study than people who weren't told to smile. Make your next book or video rental one that makes you laugh out loud; life can't be drama all the time.

- **Exercise.** I've already discussed exercise in depth, so I won't say much here. Just know that it is probably the single best way to burn off stress. Stress hormones prime you for fight or flight anyway, so you may as well give them what they want! Use those muscles and spend down that blood sugar and cortisol. Stress constricts your blood vessels, but exercise opens them back up (at least, the ones involved in the exercise). Exercise returns your system to equilibrium.

- **Sleep.** In the beginning, as we know, God divided the light from the darkness and made day and night. Was this so drive-in movies would be possible? So neon signs would look good? No! It was because there is a time to work and a time to sleep. We are meant to stop each day and take some time to rest and recharge. So don't try to steal from this time—embrace it. Sometimes our bodies have more wisdom than we do. Your body will actually tell you what it needs if you listen to it. My body certainly tells me when it is tired. For years I ignored it. I pushed and pushed and pushed and finally my body said, "I am tired of being pushed beyond reasonable limits. I am not going to cooperate any more." And it broke down. Now when my body lets me know it needs to rest, I rest! If it is sleepy, I take a nap. Sometimes ten minutes is enough to refresh me.

- **Prayer.** Prayer is simply talking to God. Some people find time with God in the morning or evening to be the best method for nurturing calm and focus, but you can try it in mini-bursts, too. Any time things start to feel overwhelming at work (or anywhere else, for that matter), put your arms on your desk, rest your head on them, close your eyes, and ask God to refresh you. Take a few deep breaths and let your mind calm down. Be very deliberate about it. Don't let your mind race through one situation after another. The goal is to pay attention to something other than what is making you feel stressed, something that actually feels peaceful. If you have a nice view out your window, take a few moments and just look at it. As you feel your system calming down, you may return to your duties, but you will do them with much greater clarity than you did previously.

- **Massage.** I admit, I'm a massage junkie. Nothing makes me feel better. And feeling good is health in itself! Massage not only relieves and tones sore muscles, but also lowers blood pressure and heart rate, releases endorphins in the brain, pushes toxins out of muscles, promotes blood flow, and increases relaxation. It may even improve immune function. We all need touch—infants who don't get touched can have stunted growth—and massage is one of the best touch therapies going.

- **Other ideas.** Unwind with music, take a warm bath by candle light or walk through a forest in autumn. You know what relaxation feels like, and you know when it's happening to you. Make relaxing on purpose part of your daily life! Above all, monitor your emotional state. Your emotions are valid, and if they feel out-of-whack, they need some TLC from you.

➤➤➤ TAKING ACTION ➤➤➤

"Be doers of the Word, and not hearers only."
(James 1:22)

Choose at least one action you can take to reduce your stress load. Write it down, *commit to it,* and begin today.

Action: _____

Right Vision

To get somewhere, you have to know where you are going. You may not know the exact route, but you at least have a goal in mind. If you are driving from St. Louis to New Orleans, you have a goal. And you have lots of means to achieve that goal, from reading maps to stopping and asking directions. On the other hand, if you just get in your car in St. Louis and drive with no idea where you're going, you probably won't get anywhere useful. You'll likely end up going in circles.

In your effort to enjoy the healthy life you deserve, you need to have a vision of your goal. What will your life be like when you are eating well, and you feel fit, comfortable, and happy? What will you look like? What kinds of activities will fill your days? Only when you have a vision of the new you can you start making the necessary plans to achieve it.

One of the most dramatic instances of this I have witnessed involved a woman I hired as a housekeeper ten years ago. The way Cindy looked when she first came to work for me made it clear how she felt about herself. She was thirty pounds overweight and put no effort into making her clothes, hair, posture, or anything else attractive. Although she did her work well, she was insecure, frequently moody, and appeared unhappy. She was also very fearful of making mistakes or disappointing people, and when she did she persecuted herself and felt guilty for days.

She was a workaholic, a classic symptom for people who feel they have no intrinsic value and can place value only in what they produce or accomplish. (And I speak from personal experience!)

It was no surprise to me to discover that Cindy was verbally abused in the earlier years of her life and made to feel as if she had no worth. But she was a very nice woman and a gifted person with a lot of potential, and I could see her spirit glinting beneath the layers it had put on over the years. She needed a vision of better things. She needed to believe that things could change for her, and eventually that is exactly what happened.

As she spent time around me and my family, Cindy started seeing that there was a different way to live. We began to do special things for her to make her feel valuable. She always liked my clothes and saw that I gave clothes away frequently to women who worked for me. She often said, "I wish I could wear your clothes." Then one day she said, "I am going to be able to wear your clothes!"

Before we achieve victory we have to transition from wishing to taking action. Cindy got a vision of what she could be, instead of believing that she always had to be what she was. Then she decided it was time to change her life. She believed she deserved more from life. She studied nutrition and, instead of going on yet another diet, changed her eating habits and knew from the beginning that it had to be a lifetime decision. Instead of working all day and then going home to a huge unhealthy meal right before bed, she began eating a good breakfast, a great lunch, and a smaller but healthy dinner. She ate lots of vegetables, lean meat, fruit, and healthy snacks. She kept getting smaller and smaller, and guess what? Cindy now wears my clothes! She looks and acts like a different person than the one I hired ten years ago.

But that's the least of it. Over the years we have watched Cindy blossom into a stylish, healthy, attractive woman who is stable and enjoys life very much. She began working for me as a housecleaner, and now she actually manages the house and helps me with many details of my life, including preparation for travel, ordering, and computer work. Best of all, I now count her as a faithful friend. I thank Cindy for being a wonderful support in my life, and for letting me share her story.

God has only one gear: forward! He has no park and no reverse. He wants you to start progressing toward your goals, but before you can do that you must get a clear image of those goals, just like Cindy did. If you are hung up on your past disappointments and keep harping on them, you are never going to escape them. Talk about your future, not your past! Talk about the new you that you are becoming. Every successful person starts off by envisioning his or her success. Now that you've learned in this book all the tools you need to become a success inside and out, to look like one and feel like one, it's time to get out the road atlas of your life, pick your destination, and slide that transmission into gear. Here are five ideas to help you pick where to go.

> *Every successful person starts off by envisioning his or her success.*

Five Ways to Develop Right Vision

1. Think (and Speak) Your Reality into Existence
"Manifesting your reality" sounds like something from a contemporary self-help course, but the concept comes straight

out of the Bible: "As he thinks in his heart, so is he" (Proverbs 23:7). I like to say it this way: "Where the mind goes, the man follows." Positive thoughts are the precursors to a positive life. On the other hand, our lives can be made miserable by anxious thoughts and negative expectations.

Most people think they cannot control their thoughts, but they can. Like anything else, it takes practice. What you think is up to you. You can choose your own thoughts and should do so carefully, since they have creative power. Thoughts become words and actions. If we don't reject bad thoughts, we will ultimately turn those thoughts into bad words and actions that are not pleasing to God. (For more help in this area, I suggest you read my book *Battlefield of the Mind*.)

We usually think our problems are the thing ruining our life, but usually it is our attitude toward them that does the ruining. As the Bible puts it, "All the days of the desponding and afflicted are made evil [by anxious thoughts and forebodings], but he who has a glad heart has a continual feast [regardless of circumstances]" (Proverbs 15:15). We all encounter people who have a great attitude despite being in trying circumstances. We also encounter those who have money and privilege to burn, yet they murmur and complain, are negative and critical, and are filled with self-pity and resentment.

We have more to do with how our lives turn out than we like to admit. Learning how to think right is mandatory for good health. Thoughts affect emotions, and they both affect the body. In order for you to be whole, you must maintain a healthy mind.

Make a decision right now that you are going to have a healthy mind. Renewing your mind will take some time and effort. You must learn new, positive ways to think. Reading God's word can help you do just that.

Another excellent practice is to create a vision of the ideal you. Carry this vision around in your head, and assume the role of the ideal you, as if you were acting in a play. Say and do the things the "ideal you" would do, instead of what the "now you" does. Soon, you will become this ideal person and won't be acting anymore. If you have never been a disciplined person but ideally you would like to be, then stop saying, "I'm just not disciplined," and begin saying, "I am a disciplined person." Say, "I look great, I feel great, and I eat right." Say, "I love to exercise and I have an abundance of energy."

Start off by doing a word sketch. Describe your ideal self's activities, physical appearance, values, and so on. Make it concrete, so it feels as real as possible. Writing down your goals helps bring them into the real world and make them solid. Keep your vision and a list of your goals somewhere handy so you can consult it periodically and see how you're doing.

Your list of goals can serve as stepping stones on your way to become your ideal self. Make sure the goals are part of a healthy vision. "I will lose twenty pounds" is not a healthy goal because it puts the focus on the scale instead of your lifestyle. "I will control my portions and get daily exercise" is a great goal, and losing five pounds this month because of that is a fine short-term goal.

2. *Manage Your Feelings*

We all have emotions, but we must learn to manage them. Emotions can be positive or negative. They can make us feel wonderful or awful. They can make us excited and enthusiastic or sad and depressed. They are a central part of being human, and that is fine. Unfortunately, most people live according to how they feel. They do what they *feel* like doing, say what they *feel* like saying, buy what they *feel* like buying, and eat what they *feel* like eating. And that is not fine, because feelings are not wisdom.

Feelings are fickle; they change frequently and without notification. Since feelings are unreliable, we must not direct our lives according to how we feel. You can be aware of your feelings and acknowledge their legitimacy without necessarily acting on them. God has given us wisdom, and we should walk in it, not emotions. Wisdom includes common sense; it involves making the choice now that you will be satisfied with later, based on your knowledge. Wisdom has discernment, prudence, discretion, and many other great qualities.

Our emotions are very important. They help us recognize how we truly feel and what we value. Good emotional health is vital for a good life. But a good life also means being able to manage our emotions, and not be managed by them. As I explained in my chapter on stress, negative emotions such as anger, lack of forgiveness, worry, anxiety, fear, resentment, and bitterness cause many physical illnesses by raising our stress level.

The healthier we are, the more stable our emotions. A healthy person can handle disappointment easier than one who is unhealthy. They can remain stable through the storms of life. But when the body is already drained, emotions cave in at the first sign of anything going wrong. When I was eating poorly, not sleeping, and living under constant stress, I was dominated by my emotions. When your emotions have been under a lot of strain, they need time to heal just like a broken arm would.

It seems to me sometimes that most of the world is mad, and the ones who aren't are sad. Things are pretty bad when people have to go to classes for "road rage." Part of this epidemic may be dietary. It doesn't occur to most people that their emotional well-being is partially dependent on what they eat. Thank God we no longer have to be like "most people." Through proper education and a desire to have a lifetime of health, we can be released from bondage. You know the old saying: "garbage in, garbage out." Eating low-quality, high-carb diets is associated with quick drops in blood sugar (hypoglycemia) which causes not only hunger but grumpiness, sadness, confusion, and related feelings.

To manage your emotions and manage your life, you need to call on Heaven's wisdom; but to have the clarity of mind to receive Heaven's wisdom, it helps to have good nutrition.

For more information on this topic, read my book *Managing Your Emotions*.

3. Assume the Best
We can quickly ruin a day with wrong thinking. Friendships are destroyed because of wrong thinking. Business deals go wrong. Marriages fail. It's so easy to concentrate on everything that is wrong with your spouse instead of what is right, and soon you want to get away from the person you are married to, when what you really want to escape is your own negative mind.

Replace suspicion and fear with trust. Trust breeds trust. Trusting others, and especially trusting God, helps keep us healthy. When we trust, we are relaxed and at rest.

This is good old common sense. Consider the following case.

You are walking down an unfamiliar street and a man comes out of his house with his pit bull growling on a leash and mutters, "What are you doing in my yard?" You think, *Who is this nutcase?*, and act angry and suspicious right back. His unfriendliness boomerangs back to him (and probably makes him unfriendlier still). On the other hand, if you are somehow able to look beyond his suspiciousness (maybe he was recently robbed?) and act extremely friendly and relaxed toward him, more often than not he will relax, too, and you'll have a friendly interaction that improves his day and yours.

Call this the "boomerang effect." Or follow the Bible and call it "reaping what you sow." Whatever you call it, it's an old rule. You get what you give.

4. Get the Small Things Right

Have you ever gone out to breakfast with somebody whose meal cost them eight dollars and watched them torture themselves over the tip? They have two one-dollar-bills in change, but they know leaving just a dollar would be chintzy. Yet do they leave two dollars? Not on your life! That would be too much. Instead, they'll waste ten minutes out of their life getting change on that second dollar so they can leave $1.50 tip and save themselves fifty cents, rather than leave an "exceptionally generous" tip of two dollars.

But what would happen if they left the full two dollars? They'd free up some valuable time—time undoubtedly worth more to them than fifty cents. And they'd make the waitress's day. Not that the actual fifty cents means much to her, either, but the message that goes along with that fifty cents means the world! It says thanks, and it says what she does has value.

Maybe this message gets lost—she may just sweep up the tip without counting—but the generous person will always be blessed. He will know instinctively that he has done the better thing. What an opportunity . . . we can increase the happiness of others and ourselves for mere pocket change!

This is just one tiny example of the many ways in which the small things we do have surprisingly powerful repercussions. Small things set the tone for our days. Going the extra mile for people—whether it's a slightly larger tip, an unexpected compliment or gift, or even holding a door for them—costs you very little, and gets you a lot.

There are many other ways to get the small things right. I've already talked about how making yourself look attractive and competent will alter how others treat you, but it will also alter how you think of yourself. If I stay in my nightgown all day and don't fix my hair, when I catch a glimpse of myself in the mirror, I don't like what I see. I see a lazy, sloppy person, and I think of myself that way. But if I dress nicely, even if I'm going to work from home all day, I feel professional, competent, and attractive and I act that way.

And, of course, if somebody stops by unexpectedly, I don't have to make excuses. I don't have to say, "Oh, you came on the one day of the year when the dishes are dirty, the house is a mess, and I'm still in my pajamas. I'm not usually like this!" *I'm not usually like this* is a line you should never utter, because it is so rarely true. If you are like this one day, you are going to be like this another day, and probably many others.

If you don't want to be "like this," make sure you're not. Do all the small things that a person of sincerity, faith, self-respect, and excellence would do, and you'll discover that you are that person! We should take good care of ourselves first for God and secondly for ourselves. I don't clean myself up and try to look my best when I'm home alone to impress others; there is nobody there to impress. I do it for the Lord and for me. I have to look at myself and I want to be pleased with what I look at.

5. Be a Part of Something Bigger Than Yourself

As I discussed in Key 1: Let God Do the Heavy Lifting, and elsewhere, you will have much more success in all your endeavors if you make them about something other than YOU. Nothing can make your vision more "right" than knowing that you are working for God's glory, and that your ultimate destination is His kingdom. There is much work to do on Earth, and a multitude of ways of carrying it forward. Whether it is working with those less fortunate than you, helping children become strong and happy adults, or spreading the Good News far and wide, nothing is more fulfilling or makes doing the right thing easier than knowing that you are part of the grandest vision of them all!

>>> TAKING ACTION >>>

"Be doers of the Word, and not hearers only."
(James 1:22)

Choose at least one action you can take to develop your vision. Write it down, *commit to it,* and begin today.

Action: _____

⊱ KEY 11 ⊰
Make It Easy

Congratulations! You have made it through all the hard parts of the book, and you are still going. You have all the tools and tips you need at your disposal to create a life of great health, reflected inside and out. If you are a person of passion, like me, you are probably chomping at the bit to launch into your new lifestyle, to embrace all of it as fast as possible. If that is the case, then my purpose in writing this book has been fulfilled.

But let me be the first to say *whoa!* Go slow. If you set down this book, pull on your sneakers, and try to start walking five miles a day while making free-range chicken stir-fries for dinner, guzzling eight glasses of water, filling your gratitude journal, and meditating at your desk each day, then you are going to be overwhelmed.

This is a case of "Do as I say, not as I do." I'm the classic example of the person who tries to do too much too fast. I tend to make quick decisions and have unrealistic expectations. I cannot tell you how many times I have started an exercise program and hurt myself because I tried to do too much. My husband, Dave, who is very patient and has exercised all his life, tries to tell me over and over to start slow, but "slow" is not in my vocabulary. If your temperament is like mine, I hope you can learn from my mistakes.

Most human beings want everything fast, but God is not in a

hurry. He is in this with you for the long haul. He will deliver you from all your bondages little by little. It takes a long time to get our lives into a mess, and it will take some time to see things turned around. Don't be too hard on yourself, especially in the beginning. You have a lot to learn and absorb. There is a reason I've asked you to take only one action for each key and not five!

The biggest favor you can do yourself is to not set the bar too high at first. If you have unrealistic expectations, you will probably end up discouraged. People who try to fix everything that is wrong in one week often give up. Remember, these changes are supposed to last a lifetime!

I have found that the secret to success in any long-term project is to make it easy. This flies in the face of what so many self-help books proclaim. "No pain, no gain." Since pain is your body's way of telling you to STOP doing something, perhaps this phrase doesn't make much sense after all. You don't need to push yourself to the limit of your capacity, unless you're training for the Olympics. You will improve simply by doing something regularly. And the only way you are going to do it regularly is if you don't mind doing it. For most of us, the rewards must clearly outweigh the inconvenience. All you care about is the outcome, and you don't get extra points for toughness or extreme willpower, so don't make things extra hard on yourself.

I am not saying that your new program will always be easy, because it won't. Any time we break old bad habits and make new ones that are good for us, it presents challenges. You will definitely have to resist the temptation to give up and be willing to press on during those times when your progress isn't going as fast as you'd like. I am saying that you can make it as easy on yourself as possible.

You can do a number of things to make your new lifestyle a relatively painless adjustment. In fact, it pays to start thinking early about the context in which you'll introduce your new habits. If you are going to start walking a mile a day, when are you going to do it? Try to pick a time when you aren't going to feel pressure to skip. ("But, Mom, I need you to take me to practice right now!") Where are you going to do it? Are you going to do it by yourself or with someone? Arranging your life so that your new healthy habits fit right in is a key to long-term commitment.

What ways can you introduce positive reinforcement into your plan? What ways can you remove temptation to fail? Are there people you can team up with who can help support your goals? Should you drop out of that dessert club you have belonged to for two years? Can you plan vacations that focus on health and fitness? Or on relaxation and spiritual refreshment? If we get serious about it, there are innumerable ways most of us can tinker with our lives to help make success easier than failure. When failure takes more work than success, it doesn't happen. That is why I know you can succeed. I believe you are on your way to great things. I'll be cheering in your corner and look forward to hearing of your victory!

> *When failure takes more work than success, it won't happen.*

Five Ways to Make Success Easy

1. Take Small Steps
Walking a mile takes about 2,000 steps. There are no other options or shortcuts. And every one of those steps is a tiny success

that brings you closer to your goal. The same is true of any other big goal. In the previous chapter I talked about the importance of setting your sights on your dreams and goals, and now I'll remind you how essential it is to break down those goals into doable steps.

If you concentrate only on your ultimate goals, it is easy to get lost halfway there. Again, think of it like driving from St. Louis to New Orleans. Your ultimate goal is New Orleans, and you have to keep in mind where you're going, but before you can start thinking about New Orleans you need to find that I-55 entrance ramp and start heading south.

Plan your short-term goals so you have something within reach to shoot for. Writing them down will give you a sense of whether or not you are on track. For example, if your ultimate goal is to walk three miles a day, five days a week, you might start off with only a half-mile three days a week. Whatever you *think* you can do. The next week, you might aim for a mile each of the three days, and so on, slowly upping your accomplishments without risking failure and disappointment. Don't make light of little victories. Small successes breed large ones. Remember, you have nothing to prove to anyone but yourself! Reaching short-term realistic goals will encourage you to press on toward the big prize.

2. Laugh at Setbacks

No matter how carefully you plan your progress, you will have setbacks. That's part of life. One of the big differences between successful and unsuccessful people is not whether they have setbacks, or even the frequency of their setbacks, but how they respond to them. Successful people are able to laugh off setbacks and get right back on the horse.

Having a bad day does not mean you have to have a bad life. Don't be like the Israelites who wanted to return to Egypt every time they had a bad day in the desert while traveling toward the Promised Land. You are being freed from the bondage of Egypt and heading toward the Promised Land of looking great and feeling great, but you will have days in the desert. Days when your program won't be as exciting as it seemed at first. Days when you feel useless. That's fine. Don't be hard on yourself on such days. Be nurturing and supportive, as you would for anyone else you love. Remind yourself that ten days forward and one day backward still gets you where you are going.

Consider writing down your victories as you have them. Keep a journal of your journey toward great health, inside and out, and record all your little successes. When you have a discouraging day or one where you feel you've done everything wrong, read your journal. You may be amazed at how far you have come.

3. Make It Convenient

If you are a busy person—and who isn't?—you will have to find ways to fit the twelve keys into your schedule. Exercising takes time. Preparing or finding healthy foods to eat takes time. Reading labels takes time. Praying takes time. Even reducing stress can take time! Fortunately, there are ways to make all these things convenient. And there is no downside to convenience, because it isn't how hard you try, it's the results that matter.

For example, don't think that to eat healthy you must never eat fast food again and only eat at the virtuous local vegetarian restaurant. All the major fast-food chains have been pressured into offering healthy alternatives, and after a few missteps, they have gotten much better about it. All offer salads with grilled chicken or other healthy options. Steer clear of fried foods and sugary drinks and you can do pretty well with fast food if you have no other choice. And supermarkets now offer everything from sushi-to-go to bags of washed salad greens, which means healthy eating does not *always* require hours in the kitchen.

Exercise is convenient when it doesn't require you to drive anywhere, deal with special equipment, or otherwise burden your day. A lap-pool in the backyard has transformed more than one couch potato into a diehard exerciser. A jog in the morning before your usual shower takes just a few minutes and can be done before anyone even knows you've left the house. Walking at work on your lunch hour or using the company fitness room requires very little "work" on your part. Choose an exercise program that is something you can do. Don't make it something expensive that is going to take two hours out of your day.

Choose a hairstyle and clothing that make you feel good about yourself yet require little maintenance on your part. You can look excellent and still be comfortable.

Choose where you live based on what will make your healthy lifestyle goals convenient, not on a prestigious neighborhood or a fantastic resale value. Can you take walks right out the front door? Is church, school, and work an easy, low-stress drive, or a teeth-grinding hour commute? Do what is simple and you will enjoy your life more!

What other ways will make healthy lifestyle choices easier than the alternatives?

4. Make It Fun

Be realistic. You will only keep doing things if you enjoy them. God wants us to enjoy life to the full. Find an exercise you *like*. Find vegetables you *like*. Don't force down lima beans if you hate them; it will only backfire.

Exercise can be fun if you combine it with socializing, shopping, or something else you already like doing. If it's something you hate and have to make yourself do, it won't last long-term.

Obviously, you only get the spiritual and health benefits of church if you enjoy going. Shop around until you find one that resonates with your beliefs and style of worship. Few things are as fun as feeling the Spirit of God move powerfully through you and the rest of the congregation.

This point is worth thinking about carefully. Keep the concept of fun in the back of your mind the whole time you work toward a healthy lifestyle, because you aren't getting healthy to make yourself miserable. The goal is to develop a life of spiritual and emotional joy, and that should be part of the payoff all along the way.

5. Reward Yourself

Don't underestimate the power of silly rewards. Treating yourself to that new pair of shoes you've wanted after you reach your first short-term goal may be a pretty transparent motivational scheme, but it still works! There's nothing wrong with making yourself feel good. The carrot works much better than the stick. And remember, it pleases God when you take care of yourself. You are worth it in His eyes.

When you lay out your short-term and long-term goals, go ahead and jot down some appropriate rewards for yourself with it. That will give you something to think about when struggling to complete that final lap in the pool or when forcing yourself to walk past the candy counter. "Just five more strokes and I'll treat myself to that new CD." Make sure the rewards are appropriate—big rewards for meeting your main goals and smaller tokens for your daily positive reinforcements. Just the knowledge that you are successfully reaching your goals may be enough motivation for you.

Celebration can be a big part of this. Celebrations and parties help give structure to your journey and let you reflect on what you've accomplished. They also let your friends and family know how important your new goals are to you—and getting their support can make all the difference.

➤➤➤ TAKING ACTION ➤➤➤

"Be doers of the Word, and not hearers only."
(James 1:22)

Choose at least one action you can take to make your healthy lifestyle extra easy on you. Write it down, *commit to it,* and begin today.

Action: _____

➤ KEY 12 ➤
Take Responsibility

One of the biggest problems in society today is that people don't want to take responsibility for their lives. They want quick fixes. Society has trained them to believe that if they have problems, somebody else is responsible. Their parents are responsible. Their spouses are responsible. Their schools or employers are responsible. The company that made the cigarettes or vehicle or junk food is responsible.

I don't like this passive mentality. Maybe your parents did feed you a lot of junk food when you were young, or never encouraged exercise. Maybe you do have the "thrifty gene" that makes you more likely to store fat than the average person. Maybe you do have a sixty-hour-a-week job with a long commute that gives you little time to make a home-cooked meal. Whatever your life is, you must make the best you can out of it.

Whatever your life is, you must make the best you can out of it.

I'm not saying you are responsible for the current state of your life. Lots of uncontrollable events occur in our lives. Sometimes we do get very bad messages in childhood. Sometimes we have bad people in our lives who hurt us. The situation you find yourself in may or may not be your fault. But it *is* your fault if you take it lying down! You do not have to stay in that bad situation. You get to make a choice. And that choice is 100 percent yours.

My parents did not teach me anything about nutrition because they did not know anything about it. Does that give me a free pass to eat poorly? No, I had to take responsibility and educate myself in these areas. A lot of people in my family's bloodline were overweight. It would have been easy to say, "It runs in my genes." Although body structure is inherited, it is not an excuse to remain unhealthy.

No matter how you got to where you find yourself today, don't let it be an excuse to stay there. I had many excuses and reasons for my poor health, bad attitude, and unbalanced life. As long as I offered excuses, I never made progress.

Taking responsibility for where we are is a must in making progress. Shifting the blame keeps us trapped. It may put off a little guilt in the short term, but in the long run it just prolongs our misery.

A woman who works for me has a big bone structure. If you stand her and her mother side by side, they look exactly alike. This woman cannot do anything about her bone structure, but she takes good care of herself. She's in shape, looks good, and nobody even notices that her frame is a bit larger. She could make excuses and let herself go to pieces, chalking it up to genes, or fate, but instead she lives responsibly. Her reward for being responsible is that she is happy and gets the fullness out of life.

The Power of Free Will

It would be so easy if God had not given us free will. We could wander through the days like robots, eating the fruit that falls into our hands and waiting for the next thing to happen to us.

But He did give us free will, which gives us tremendous responsibility but also the possibility of total joy and fulfillment.

God will give you all the tools you need on Earth to reach spiritual completion. But it's up to you to take up those tools and put them to work restoring your health and renovating His Temple for Him. He can make it as easy on you as possible—and, in writing this book, I've tried to help by giving you some useful information, guidance, and tips—but He can't do the work for you. The work is an essential part of the fulfillment, an essential part of the process of freeing your soul from bondage. When you are in the depths of self-pity, free will can feel awful, a pressure and responsibility you just don't want. But once you make the commitment to maintain your body and soul as you should, to be a person of excellence and power, you discover that free will is your most valuable possession.

This is why you must avoid self-pity at all costs. Self-pity is an emotion that feeds on itself and steals your power. You need power to become the person you were meant to be, and you cannot be pitiful and powerful at the same time. I had a major problem with self-pity in my earlier years, and not until I stopped feeling sorry for myself did I start making progress.

We feel better about ourselves when we approach life boldly, ready to be accountable and responsible. You don't have to hide from anything. You can do whatever you need to do in life. You can look healthy and attractive. You can feel great inside and out. You can live a life that keeps you fit and happy into old age. It's all up to you. Through God you are ready for anything. Confront your life head on and never turn back!

One Way to Take Responsibility for Your Life

Up until now I've given you five options for implementing each of the twelve keys to enjoying your life fully. Now, right at the last key, I'm changing things up. When it comes to taking responsibility for your own life, there is no wiggle room, no extra choices for ways to get started. The time has come to be very honest with yourself and with God. You either do it or you don't. Using everything you have learned in this book, you can easily break your old habits and transform. Make the decision to do so. When you have a moment of privacy, take a deep breath, clear your head, and repeat this phrase:

"I am responsible for my own life. No one can take charge of it but me. If I am unhappy or unhealthy, I know I have the power to change that. I have all the help and knowledge I need, and with God's hand today I start becoming the person of excellence I have always known I could be."

Congratulations. Thanks for taking this journey with me, and blessings on you for the exciting and wondrous journey you are just beginning.

>>> TAKING ACTION >>>

"Be doers of the Word, and not hearers only."
(James 1:22)

Choose to take charge of your life. Write down your decision, *commit to it,* and begin today.

Action: _____

Epilogue

Practice What You Preach:
Modeling Self-Respect for the Next Generation

Look Great, Feel Great is about transforming yourself into a person of joy and excellence, a person whose health and vitality shows beautifully in who you are and all that you do. One thing I have talked about a lot is the way our bad habits are practically forced on us by a culture that makes bad habits more convenient and encouraging than their healthy alternatives. A lot of this starts early in our lives. If you have made it to this point and freed yourself from those bad cultural bonds, you may realize the problem: Coming up right behind you is a whole new generation that needs saving, too.

If there is one thing sadder than the abuses fostered by adults in an American culture that disdains health, it is the terrible impact this has on our kids. When we think of childhood, we can barely separate it from the idea of activity. Childhood is about running around, playing games on the lawn or in the park, walking or riding bikes to the store, swimming in pools and ponds, and playing sports. But if you haven't checked in with today's schools recently, you may be in for a shock, because that isn't always what childhood is about anymore.

Today's kids face an obesity epidemic. The number of overweight kids and teens has tripled since the 1970s, from five percent to fifteen percent, and is rising faster than ever. Obesity is very difficult on kids. Not only does it come with serious social and emotional baggage, but it also predisposes them to a life of poor health. Overweight kids run twice the risk of developing high blood pressure, heart disease, and Type-2 diabetes. Type-2 diabetes used to be known as adult-onset diabetes because we never saw it in kids. Not anymore. Now we see signs of artery damage in three-year-olds who eat the typical American diet. Three-year-olds! These little ones have barely learned how to talk and we are saddling them with a lifelong health problem. A third of today's kids will develop diabetes during their lifetimes. We can't let this go on.

Don't think that the problem disappears in adulthood, either. Overweight kids find it difficult to turn things around when they grow up. Their bodies and minds "learn" to be overweight. In fact, one study of female Harvard graduates showed that their risk for diseases such as cancer and heart disease directly related to their level of exercise as adolescents. If other studies back this up, then exercise during the teen years may be the single most important way to prevent disease later in life. In a way that's great news, because it means that as a parent or teacher you have the chance to give a gift that keeps on giving, long after your children have left the nest.

You can guess the reasons for kids' weight problems because they are no different from the factors affecting adults. Poor eating habits are a problem, but the worst culprit is good old lack of exercise. Weight Watchers estimates that overeating is responsible for thirty percent of the problem, while lack of exercise accounts for fifty percent, and a 2002 government study concluded that the only way to fix the problem is to focus on exercise.

Will that be easy? Absolutely not. As anyone who has raised teens can tell you, it's easier to wrestle a bear than convince teens to change their habits. If you want to instill good habits in teens, start working on it when they're young, innocent, and still believe you know a thing or two. If you live in a neighborhood where kids can play outside with their friends, you have already won half the battle. But in too many neighborhoods kids *can't* play safely outside. The average child in America watches three hours of TV every day. Not only is that three hours of sitting, but studies show that you burn even fewer calories watching TV than you do *sitting still!* Worse, those three hours per day add up to 10,000 commercials per year, the majority of which are for junk food or fast food. That's quite a double-whammy: Not only does TV keep your kids from exercising, but at the same time it teaches them to want lousy food.

The easiest solution is to limit your kids' TV viewing. Make them play or do something constructive. Get them to use their minds and do something that gets them moving. They'll be in a better mood that night. If your child is one who likes to participate in organized sports, great. If not, don't push it on her or you'll have a sports hater for life. There are a million other ways to make exercise fun and easy that don't involve round balls and coaches.

One of the best ways you can instill a lifelong love of exercise in your kids is to start a tradition of family walks when they are young. Even three-year-olds can be pretty good walkers. By taking family walks, you *model* good behavior for your kids, which is essential. "Do as I say, not as I do" just doesn't cut it with kids. Kids are smart and take their cues from you. If you walk, and they walk, then you don't need to lecture them on why exercise is important. It goes without saying.

The benefits of family walks go beyond this, too. You'll find that the "down time" during walks is a natural chance to talk about things and find out what is going on in your kids' lives. It's great bonding time.

As kids get into their teen years, they'll be less inclined to walk with you, but there are plenty of ways to keep them active. The neighborhoods where kids can still walk to school are far too rare these days, but if you are fortunate enough to live in one, be sure to take advantage of it. At the very least, they can walk to the bus stop. Try to come up with chores that involve exercise: mowing the lawn, raking leaves, and walking the dog are three good examples. If you need something from the local convenience store a mile down the road—that has "teen mission" written all over it.

Making exercise a part of kids' home life is more important than ever because schools just aren't helping on this front. Don't blame the schools—they are more cash-strapped than ever. Phys Ed is one of the first programs to get the axe when budget crunches hit. What else could they cut? English? Recesses are also going by the wayside. As they cut closer and closer to the bone, schools are desperately trying to hold on to their role of taking care of kids' minds, leaving kids' bodies completely up to parents and Little League.

That's bad enough, but something much scarier is going on in our schools. If you haven't heard about it yet, let me be the first to sound the alarm. Desperate for money, schools are welcoming soft drink vending machines into their halls. Soda companies pay as much as $100,000 a year for the exclusive rights to get their products into schools because they know that a teen consumer is usually hooked for life.

What does too much soda do to a young body? For starters, it pumps hundreds of empty calories in—calories that add pounds without nutrition. With thirty grams or more of sugar per serving, soda is the fast track to diabetes. But the nasty impact of soda goes even further. Soda is full of phosphoric acid, which must be buffered in the digestive tract. Calcium is the best way to do this. Where does your body get that calcium? From your bones. A steady diet of soda leaches calcium out of young bones at the worst possible time: half of bone mass is developed during the teen years. This helps explain why teenage girls who drink soda are three times more likely to suffer bone fractures than girls who don't drink soda.

Of course, most teen girls *do* drink soda, which may be behind the alarming results of a recent Mayo Clinic study. The study found that, over the past thirty years, girls' rate of wrist and forearm fractures has gone up *fifty-six percent!* The rate among boys has gone up, too. The reason is probably that teens are now drinking less milk and more soda than they used to. Kids should get at least four servings of dairy per day. Do yours? If your kids don't like milk, cheese, or yogurt, other good sources of calcium include greens, broccoli, and sardines. ("Awesome, Mom, our favorites!")

In addition to limiting your kids' soda intake, you can do wonders for their bones with strength training. Doctors used to believe that strength training could hurt developing bodies, but now we know that moderate routines can have a positive, safe impact on teens. In fact, the benefits of strength training in girls blow away what we see in adults. One study of girl figure skaters who averaged ten years of age found that just two simple strength workouts per week increased their strength by sixty-seven percent, their vertical jump by thirteen percent, and improved their scores in competition. Of course, it also did wonders for their self-confidence.

Self-confidence may be the key when discussing weight issues with teens. So often the two go together. Which is the chicken and which is the egg hardly matters. Do kids watch TV and play video games, get overweight, and then get teased and feel bad about themselves? Or does teasing and lack of self-esteem lead them to stay inside more, eat to compensate, and gain weight? Either way, what you need to do is get them on a better track with better habits *and* better self-confidence. What you *don't* want to do is make them feel worse about their weight—they already feel bad enough.

To get results without making a big issue of it, I recommend taking the focus off weight and putting it on fitness. Don't tell your teen, "You need to lose weight!" Instead, introduce him to the basics of fitness and nutrition. Teens are interested in how their bodies work and like to learn. Have them read some of the chapters in this book and they'll be off to a great start. If you are modeling the behavior you want them to emulate, all the better. Go on family hikes or after-dinner walks that get kids walking without singling them out as the goats. Whatever you do, don't compare them to their older siblings. That's a sure way to sink self-esteem.

Eating Disorders

If the bad news is that teen obesity is skyrocketing, the good news is that it is on everyone's radar now. So are eating disorders, the flip side of teen food issues. Ten million females in the United States have anorexia or bulimia, as do a million males. The disorders often arise in adolescence. Anorexia is like dieting that has gone out of control. The person resists eating and wastes away until serious health problems result, including slowed heart rate and dangerously low blood pressure, osteoporosis, muscle loss, dehydration, and hair loss. Bulimia, which is characterized by cycles of eating and purging (usually through vomiting) can result in rupture of the stomach or esophagus, tooth decay (from stomach acid), and intestinal problems.

Rarely will you find one single cause of eating disorders, but media messages are definitely a factor. Our culture glorifies thinness, and magazines aimed at young women are some of the worst offenders. Girls who are pressured or ridiculed about their size or weight are more likely to develop eating disorders, as are girls who have been physically or sexually abused, or have high-stress lives and little control over them.

Signs of eating disorders include intense weight loss, preoccupation with food, depression or low self-esteem, and sometimes an obsession with exercise (as a way of making one's body "disappear"). If you recognize these symptoms in a child you know, pay close attention. Treatment for eating disorders usually takes some time and involves psychotherapy, group support, and nutritional counseling. Severe cases can require hospitalization until eating is normalized.

The best solution, of course, is to prevent eating disorders from getting started in the first place by teaching kids healthy body images and lifestyles. Here are some ways to do just that.

Ten Ways to Put Fitness and Self-Esteem in Kids' Lives

1. Model Good Behavior

Everything you do is monitored *closely* by the little eyes in your house. If you stay active, get regular exercise, lay off the TV, and eat healthy meals, your kids will too—even if it doesn't seem like it at first.

2. Increase Your School Budget

When schools are forced to slash their budgets, Phys Ed goes first. After-school programs soon follow. Get your town to support its schools. Healthy schools make a healthy community. If you want to get really active, encourage schools to introduce more cooperative and fewer competitive sports. Many students, especially girls, are turned off by sports that emphasize winners and losers. I'd love to see coaches get more training in teaching personal fitness and have them introduce kids to that, as well as getting out the volleyball nets.

3. Can the Soda

Replace at least part of your teen's soda consumption with milk and you will help guarantee strong bones for life. Or substitute a juice-and-seltzer mix for straight soda or fruit juice. You cut the calories in half and get them less hooked on the taste of sugar. If your kids drink a lot of whole milk and have a weight issue, switch to two percent milk. If you already drink two percent, switch to one percent. Your taste buds will adjust quickly and you won't miss the needless fat.

4. Get 'em While They're Young
The earlier you start kids on healthy behavior, the more natural it will seem to them. By the time they are teens, it's hard to make them switch habits. But even if you start when they are teens, this is far better than waiting until adulthood, because most of the body's important development is complete by age eighteen.

5. Get Them Moving
If teens participate three times per week in aerobic exercise—such as walking, running, biking, swimming, or high school sports—they are in great shape. If they add a couple of bouts of strength training per week, they will be strong, fit, and secure. Don't let them push it to adult levels, but moderate workouts can be a teen's best friend.

6. Pay Attention to Breakfast and Lunch
I wouldn't be surprised if we could nip the childhood obesity epidemic in the bud by making kids sit down and eat a real breakfast before heading out the door. How many kids just chomp a Pop Tart on the way to the bus? This does nobody any favors. Metabolism crashes, resulting in fatigue, inability to concentrate, and fat storage. Studies show overwhelming differences between kids who have breakfast and those who don't. Give your children a real breakfast and they perform much better—physically and mentally. Meanwhile, school lunches

are going in two directions. Some schools are making a real effort to provide healthier meals. Others can't deal with it and are letting fast-food chains take over the cafeterias. We may as well declare war on our children! Find out what your kid is eating for lunch.

7. Don't Use Pressure

Make a teen feel bad for the way she eats and you are asking for real trouble. At best, resentment. At worst, eating disorders. Focus on fitness and healthy food instead, and make it a family priority, not a boot camp for one kid.

Our moms meant well when they made us clear our plates, but often this instilled poor habits in us. "Clean your plate or no dessert" we were told—which made us stuff ourselves just to get to the cake, and then somehow force that in, too. Ugh! If you always eat until your plate is clear, rather than until you are full, you lose the ability to judge when you have eaten enough. Kids are very good at eating what they need. Rather than force them to eat a certain amount or a particular vegetable, provide them with lots of healthy options (and few junky ones), don't use food as a reward, and let them make their own decisions about what to eat from the healthy variety you provide.

8. Let Them Sleep In

Teens aren't being lazy when they stumble from their bedrooms at ten o'clock; they are responding to their biological needs. Many new studies show that teens need one to two hours more sleep than adults do. If teens get less than nine hours of sleep a night, they start to perform worse. They get worse grades, are in more car accidents, and are more likely to develop depression or ADHD.

9. Set Up for Success

Make sure your kids' environment is one that makes exercise easy. A home with nothing going on outside, but a big-screen TV inside with every video game known to man does not encourage exercise. If basketball hoops, volleyball nets, and tennis racquets are around, they'll get used. If money is an issue, there are lots of parks that offer free courts, swimming, and paths.

10. Make Vacations Count

No matter where you live, vacations can be a great time to introduce teens to new exercises that may hook them for life. This could be snorkeling in Florida, horseback riding in Colorado, or skiing in Vermont. When exercise becomes cool, it goes down a lot easier. Even New York City can be a great exercise town: walk from museum to museum and you'll have done many miles by the time you collapse on your hotel bed that night. Most theme parks involve a lot of walking. Closer to home, events like county fairs keep kids walking all night without them even realizing it. (Just watch out for the cotton candy!)

Appendix A

Let Me Hear From You

I want to know about your success! I don't write books for myself. I don't sit in my study in the evening looking them over and saying, "Good point, Joyce! Nice sentence!" No, I write books to reach out. To establish relationships with you and other good people like you.

A relationship is not a one-way street. It's two-way. So for our relationship to move forward, I need to hear from you! Your success is so very important to me. I want to hear your inspiring story and perhaps share it with others. I welcome your prayer requests, too.

You can reach me at:

Joyce Meyer Ministries
P.O. Box 655
Fenton, MO 63026
636-349-0303
www.joycemeyer.org

In Canada:

Joyce Meyer Ministries—
   Canada
Lambeth Box 1300
London, ON N6P 1T5
636-349-0303

In Australia:

Joyce Meyer Ministries—
   Australia
Locked Bag 77
Mansfield Delivery Centre
Queensland 4122
07-3349-1200

In England:

Joyce Meyer Ministries
P.O. Box 1549
Windsor
SL4 1GT
(0) 1753-831102

Appendix B

An Ounce of Prevention:
A Daily Self-Maintenance Checklist

Be an investor, not a gambler. You can ignore all the little things that contribute to a lifetime of health and hope that you are blessed in old age, or you can invest in your future by putting a little time each day into personal upkeep, knowing that you'll get to "spend" all that time, plus interest, throughout a healthy, long life. Use this checklist each day to keep yourself on track. You can photocopy it from this book or devise your own.

Date _____

Daily Tasks

Nutrition

❏ 6–10 glasses water
❏ 5 servings fruits & vegetables
❏ 2 servings healthy protein (fish, poultry, eggs, beans, etc.)
❏ Multivitamin or supplement

Hygiene

❏ Brushed
❏ Flossed!
❏ Skin clean & moisturized
❏ Hair & nails clean & attractive

Lifestyle

❏ Exercise: _____ (activity and duration)
❏ Dressed in a way I am proud of
❏ Shoes comfortable & supportive
❏ Got a full night's sleep

Spirit

❏ Reduced or avoided stress today: _____ (how?)
❏ Renewed my spirit today: _____ (how?)
❏ Did something for someone else: _____ (what?)
❏ Thought about my long-term goals

General Reminders

Protect your back when lifting • Avoid excessive sun • Don't smoke • Don't strain your eyes in bad light or by using incorrect glasses • Smile and laugh often • Don't do anything in excess • Get yearly checkups • Wash your hands frequently to prevent infection • Get six-month dental cleanings • Pray about everything throughout the day • Enjoy your life

Appendix C

Quick-Fix Emergency Sheet

Maintaining the physical and spiritual glow that comes from great health is a matter of sticking to your twelve-key plan each day. But watch out for those moments of weakness. The feelings pop up every day, and we all experience them. Getting yourself through those moments of weakness is your key to enjoying a healthy life now. Photocopy this Quick-Fix Emergency Sheet, carry it with you, and when you feel yourself weaken in any of your twelve key areas during the day, pull it out and get yourself back on track. (*Remember, these are quick-fixes for crisis moments; read each chapter in the twelve-key plan to achieve your full potential.*)

Key 1. Let God Do the Heavy Lifting

Feeling: *I can't do it! I'm not strong enough!*

Quick-Fix: • Stop what you're doing and clear your mind. Remind yourself that you don't have to do it alone. Ask God to take charge and act through you. Then go back to your task.

Key 2. Learning to Love Your Body

Feeling: *I'm fat/ugly/old/whatever!*

Quick-Fix: • Immediately treat yourself well. Buy a single flower, put it in a vase by your bed, and enjoy its beauty. Remind yourself: "I'm created in the image of God. God loves me and I love myself."

Key 3. Mastering Metabolism

Feeling: *I'm a slug! My metabolism is in a coma!*

Quick-Fix: • Drink a glass of cold water (raises metabolism thirty percent).
       • Eat a breakfast with protein and whole grains.
       • Don't skip meals!
       • Exercise vigorously for ten minutes.

Key 4. Exercise

Feeling: *I'm overweight.*

              I'm grumpy/sleepy/sad.

Quick-Fix: • Go for a walk or run. Ride a bike or swim. Nothing strenuous. Daily *moderate* exercise cuts your risk of heart disease, diabetes, and stroke in half and melts twenty pounds a year off your frame. It also relieves mild depression and makes you more productive.
       • If you can't fit in a walk, stretch at your desk for ten minutes.

Key 5. Balanced Eating

Feeling: *Burger and fries sure would be easy for lunch!*

Ahhh! Pasta!

Quick-Fix: • One meal at a time, you can make right choices. When wavering between a healthy and unhealthy choice, call on the Holy Spirit to help you make the right choice. Now, say out loud "I have self-control and I will eat what's best for me."

• Maximize your veggies: get the fast-food salad; or the sandwich with lots of veggies, tuna or turkey, and no cheese; or the veggie-lover's pizza.

Key 6. Water Your Life

Feeling: *I'm lethargic; I need food or caffeine!*

Quick-Fix: • The run-down feeling of dehydration is often mistaken for hunger or low energy. Drink a full glass of water immediately, wait fifteen minutes, and see if you feel better.

• Drink a glass of water before every meal.

• Keep a bottle of water with you at all times.

Key 7. Mindful Eating

Feeling: *I just need something to munch on while I work/drive/watch TV.*

I think I'll have some more!

Finished. Must be time for dessert!

Quick-Fix: • Keep healthy, easy snack food at arm's reach: baby carrots, protein bars, broccoli florets, fruit, and frozen juice popsicles are good choices.

• Whenever you lift food to your mouth, ask yourself, "Does this taste good? Do I need it?" Eat only necessary food.

- Never take seconds. You don't need them. Instead, put down your fork, stand up, and walk around.

Key 8. Curb Your Spiritual Hunger

Feeling: *Food is the only thing that interests me.*

Quick-Fix: • You are mistaking spiritual hunger for physical hunger. If you are feeling bored, lonely, or depressed, food won't fill that void. Instead, close your eyes and picture God's love pouring into you. Now think about how silly that snack food seems.

Key 9. De-Stress

Feeling: *I'm so frustrated and upset by work/him/her/life that I can't relax!*

Quick-Fix: • Close your eyes, lie down or put your head down on your desk, and count to sixty, picturing each number in your mind as you count it. Breathe deeply while you do this. Remind yourself that this, too, shall pass.
- Go for a walk or run or swim. Take a bath or listen to soothing music.

Key 10. Right Vision

Feeling: *It's pointless! I'm so far away from my goals!*

Quick-Fix: • Successful lives are made of successful days. Look how far you've come. Take a moment, go somewhere quiet, and envision the life you want. What can you do today—just today—to get one step closer to that life?

Key 11. Make It Easy

Feeling: *I don't have time to exercise/cook/read this book!*

Quick-Fix: • You don't get credit for how hard you work, so take shortcuts to health whenever possible.

        • Use a treadmill or stationary bike while you watch TV. Use the stairs instead of the elevator. Take the first parking space you see and walk a few extra yards.

        • Buy pre-washed salad greens, pre-chopped veggies, melons, and pineapples, pre-cooked shrimp, and other healthy foods that require no preparation. Nobody likes prep work!

        • Reading this book and learning its tips will give you more time to enjoy a healthy life, not less. You can't afford not to read it!

Key 12. Take Responsibility

Feeling: *I'd be fit and happy if only my parents/genes/life hadn't messed me up!*

Quick-Fix: • You may not be responsible for the events in your past that led you to your current situation. But you are responsible if you stay there! You have a choice. Say to yourself right now, "No one can take charge of my life but me. With God's help, I have the power to change. Today I become the person of excellence I have always known I could be."

Appendix D

Your Personal 12 Keys

Use this page to help yourself keep track of—and stick to—the twelve behaviors you have chosen to adopt in order to meet your lifestyle goals.

Key	Behavior, Habit, or Practice
1. Getting God's Help	
2. Accepting Your Body	
3. Mastering Metabolism	
4. Exercise	
5. Balanced Eating	
6. Water	
7. Mindful Eating	
8. Spiritual Nourishment	
9. Reducing Stress	
10. Long-Term Goals	
11. A Supportive Structure	
12. Taking Responsibility	

Bibliography

Agatston, Arthur. *The South Beach Diet*. Emmaus, PA: Rodale, 2003.

The Alternative Advisor. Alexandria, Virginia: Time-Life, 1997.

Atkins, Robert. *Dr. Atkins New Diet Revolution*. New York: Harper-Collins, 2002.

Bailey, Covert. *Smart Exercise*. Boston, MA: Houghton Mifflin, 1994.

Boston Women's Health Book Collaborative. *Our Bodies, Ourselves*. New York: Simon and Schuster, 1998.

Colbert, Don. *What Would Jesus Eat?* Nashville, TN: Thomas Nelson, 2002.

Cooper, Kenneth. *Faith-Based Fitness*. Nashville, TN: Thomas Nelson, 1995.

Dement, William. *The Promise of Sleep*. New York: Delacorte, 1999.

Evans, Mark. *Mind Body Spirit*. London: Hermes House, 2002.

Foods That Harm, Foods That Heal. Pleasantville, NY: Reader's Digest, 1997.

Hiser, Elizabeth. *The Other Diabetes*. New York: William Morrow, 1999.

Kalb, Claudia. "Faith and Healing." *Newsweek*, November 10, 2003, pp. 44–56.

Merck Manual of Medical Information, Second Home Edition. New York: Pocket Books, 2003.

Nelson, Miriam. *Strong Women Stay Young*. New York: Bantam, 1997.

"Overcoming Obesity." *Time*, June 7, 2004.

Sansone, Leslie. *Walk Away the Pounds*. New York: Warner, 2005.

Sapolsky, Robert. *Why Zebras Don't Get Ulcers*. New York: W.H. Freeman, 1998.

Schmid, Randolphe. "Stress Found to Activate Enzyme That Impairs Memory." Associated Press, October 29, 2004.

Tanner, Lindsey. "Walking May Keep Older Minds Sharp." Associated Press, September 22, 2004.

Weil, Andrew. *Eating Well for Optimum Health*. New York: Knopf, 2000.

Willet, Walter. *Eat, Drink, and Be Healthy*. New York: Free Press, 2001.

About the Author

JOYCE MEYER is one of the world's leading practical Bible teachers. A #1 *New York Times* bestselling author, she has written more than seventy inspirational books, including *The Confident Woman, I Dare You,* the entire Battlefield of the Mind family of books, her first venture into fiction with *The Penny,* and many others. She has also released thousands of audio teachings as well as a complete video library. Joyce's *Enjoying Everyday Life®* radio and television programs are broadcast around the world, and she travels extensively conducting conferences. Joyce and her husband, Dave, are the parents of four grown children and make their home in St. Louis, Missouri.

Joyce Meyer Ministries
U.S. & Foreign Office Addresses

Joyce Meyer Ministries
P.O. Box 655
Fenton, MO 63026
USA
(636) 349-0303
www.joycemeyer.org

Joyce Meyer Ministries—Canada
Lambeth Box 1300
London, ON N6P 1T5
CANADA
1-800-727-9673

Joyce Meyer Ministries—Australia
Locked Bag 77
Mansfield Delivery Centre
Queensland 4122
AUSTRALIA
(07) 3349 1200

Joyce Meyer Ministries—England
P.O. Box 1549
Windsor SL4 1GT
UNITED KINGDOM
01753 831102

Joyce Meyer Ministries—South Africa
P.O. Box 5
Cape Town 8000
SOUTH AFRICA
(27) 21-701-1056

COMING IN APRIL 2009!

We all have challenges or dreams that at times seem impossible. In NEVER GIVE UP!, Joyce Meyer provides a toolbox full of steps that will help you succeed in realizing your dreams. Packed with examples of people who relentlessly pursued their goals, the book profiles nearly fifty individuals who succeeded against all odds. From the builder of the Brooklyn Bridge to the mother who lost her only daughter at Virginia Tech, we meet people who have faced tragic circumstances and prevailed. Joyce reminds us that with God, nothing is impossible. By the time you finish reading, you'll want to revive your dream and start on the path for making it come true.

Books by Joyce Meyer

New Day, New You Devotional
I Dare You
The Penny
The Power of Simple Prayer
The Everyday Life Bible (hardcover or bonded leather)
The Confident Woman
Look Great, Feel Great
Battlefield of the Mind*
Battlefield of the Mind Devotional
Battlefield of the Mind for Teens
Battlefield of the Mind for Kids
Approval Addiction
Ending Your Day Right
21 Ways to Finding Peace and Happiness
The Secret Power of Speaking God's Word
Seven Things That Steal Your Joy
Starting Your Day Right
Beauty for Ashes (revised edition)
How to Hear from God*
Knowing God Intimately
The Power of Forgiveness
The Power of Determination
The Power of Being Positive
The Secrets of Spiritual Power
The Battle Belongs to the Lord
The Secrets to Exceptional Living
Eight Ways to Keep the Devil Under Your Feet
Teenagers Are People Too!
Filled with the Spirit
Celebration of Simplicity

Joyce Meyer Spanish Titles

Las Siete Cosas Que Te Roban el Gozo
(Seven Things That Steal Your Joy)
Empezando Tu Dia Bien (Starting Your Day Right)

*Study Guide available for this title.

Books by Dave Meyer

Life Lines